Your Sales Management Guru's Guide to:

Creating High-Performance Sales Compensation Plans

Praise for Your Sales Management Guru's Guide

"Ken Thoreson has hit a home run the *Your Sales Management Guru's Guide* series. If you want to take your sales team to the next level, read these books!" **- Jeb Blount, CEO of SalesGravy.com and Author of *People Buy You: The Real Secret to What Matters Most in Business* and *Power Principles***

"If you're a crazy-busy sales manager and constantly worried about reaching your revenue goals, follow Ken Thoreson's savvy advice to create a high-performance sales organization." **- Jill Konrath, Author of *SNAP Selling and Selling to Big Companies***

"Your Sale Management Guru's Guide is the most practical how-to book on the topic of recruiting top sales talent that I've read." **- Roberto (Bob) F. Sanchez, Managing Partner, SunGard Consulting Services and former CEO & Managing Partner of Sales Performance International**

"Ken's series of books are jammed packed with processes, systems and ideas that can be easily implemented for immediate impact."**- Brett Clay, Author of *Selling Change: 101+ Secrets for Growing Sales by Leading Change***

Praise for Your Sales Management Guru's Guide

"No fluff, no theory, no cheerleading, just substance. In his series of *Your Sales Management Guru's Guide* books, Ken Thoreson delivers solid, practical, actionable guidance for sales management success. From crafting a vision to maximizing the productivity of weekly sales meetings, Ken provides concrete recommendations that sales executives can begin applying immediately to make a positive difference in their teams' performance. " **- Tom Pick, Social Media Consultant and *Webbiquity* blog author.**

"Ken Thoreson's Your Sales Management Guru's books are among the best sales management books I have read." **- Thomas J. Winninger, CPAE, founder of the Winninger Institute for Market Growth Strategies.**

"Quick, ready-to-use sales management tools that are right on target for today's new 21st Century sales environment. Now more than ever, sales leadership and sales management are critical components to organizational success. Effectively executing that role is essential. These tools are an invaluable asset to anyone who has responsibility for organizational sales success." **- Frank Chamberlain, International Sales Consultant and Trainer, President of Resource Technologies, Inc.**

"Ken Thoreson applies his in-depth experience to help sales leaders do the things which need to be done - consistently and persistently. If you are serious about becoming the very best sales leader that you possibly can become, I urge you to read Ken Thoreson's words of wisdom – and then read them again." **- Jonathan Farrington, CEO of Top Sales Associates, Chairman of The jf Corporation and the creator of Top Sales World.**

Your Sales Management Guru's Guide to:

Creating High-Performance Sales Compensation Plans

by Ken Thoreson
"Your Sales Management Guru"

$ales Gravy

P R E S S

Sales Gravy Press
The Sales Book Publisher™
P.O. Box 1389
Thomson, GA 30824

Published by Sales Gravy Press
Printed in the United States of America

Cover Design: Dave Blaker

First Edition

ISBN-13: 978-1-935602-11-8

Table of Contents

Introduction   xiii

Acknowledgements   xviii

Chapter 1   Getting Started   1

Chapter 2   Determining Metrics for an
             Effective Compensation Plan   25

Chapter 3   Choosing a Type of
             Sales Compensation Plan   35

Chapter 4   Incorporating Incentive Programs   45

Chapter 5   One-to-One Tools for
             Driving Successful Results   55

Chapter 6   Five Steps to Building
             A Compensation Plan   65

Chapter 7   Final Words   79

Appendix A   Compensation Plan Assessment Tool   85

Appendix B   Senior Account Executive Job
             Description and Commission Plan   91

Appendix C   Compensation Committee Tools   95

Appendix D   Examples of Compensation Agreements   101

Appendix E   Key Responsibilities and Additional
             Compensation Plan Tools, Examples
             and Concepts   123

About the Author   133

Introduction

In my long experience as a sales manager, I found that what I always needed most were ideas. In my 13 years as a consultant, I've found that my clients are always looking for ideas as well. I also found I never had enough time to wait for the idea to "pop into my brain" and that is why I have created this book. The goal of *The Sales Management Guru's Guide to Creating High Performance Sales Compensation Plans* and our other titles — is to give you ideas (quickly and easily) for developing a great sales organization — and, ultimately, boosting your company's revenues.

No question: Sales management is a tough job. You've got to build and lead a sales team, you've got to report to upper management, you're responsible to your peers and your customers — and, in many cases, to your company's vendors as well. This book is designed to help you address all those issues.

At Acumen Management, we know that sales leaders need ideas, concepts and tools to help them establish winning sales organizations — and we also know that they don't have much time. *The Sales Management Guru's Guide to Creating High Performance Sales Compensation Plans* designed to provide you with a quick read that's packed with plenty of proven tools and real-world recommendations.

The key to a successful compensation plan is aligning the compensation plan to the organizations strategic objectives. In this book I have described both the strategic and tactical aspects of designing, testing, rolling out and measuring the effectiveness of your sales compensation plans. I cover why compensation is strategic and secrets of creating compensation plans that pay for performance and build a culture of success.

We've divided our advice into seven key categories:

Chapter 1   Getting Started

Chapter 2   Determining Metrics for an Effective
             Compensation Plan

Chapter 3   Choosing a Type of Sales Compensation Plan

Chapter 4   Incorporating Incentive Programs

Chapter 5   One-to-One Tools for Driving Successful
             Results

Chapter 6   Five Steps to Building a Compensation Plan

Chapter 7   Final Words on Sales Leadership
             Compensation

Within those chapters, you'll learn the important strategic issues facing sales leaders when creating compensation plans and the tactical steps that must be taken for effective design, roll out and management. Be sure to read the special Appendix's A-E where I have included samples of Compensation Plan Assessment Tools, Sample Compensation Plans, Compensation Agreements, Roll Out Plans, and Salesperson Goal Sheets.

Want more detail on strategic sales leadership? See the Sales Management Guru's other guides:

- The Sales Management Guru's Guide to Leading High Performance Sales Team
- The Sales Management Guru's Guide to Recruiting a High Performance Sales Team
- The Sales Management Guru's Ultimate Handbook for Sales Managers

All are available on our Web site (www. AcumenManagement.com), where you can also purchase five hours of sales management training on DVDs and the on-line Interactive Sales Management Tool Kit.

Our Web site also includes many free white papers and videos. And you will find more free and timely insights on our blog:

www.YourSalesManagementGuru.com.

Acknowledgements

After more than 25 years of working and consulting in sales management environments, I have so many individuals to acknowledge who have influenced my life and philosophies. Some have impacted my personal life, others my professional life and still others, both.

I'd like to start by acknowledging my mentors Sam Hagerman, a Boy Scout Camp Director in the early days of my life, as well as David Keene, President of Versyss, who offered me the opportunity to become a VP of Sales and gain the perspective of leading a major organization. There were countless individuals that I have worked with in my professional life that put up with me; each of you, I trust, knows your impact. Thank you.

In addition, I would like to thank my personal friends Dennis Pottebaum and Larry Decklever who continually offered positive reinforcement and support during my early days of becoming an entrepreneur. Also, Karen Winner, thank you for all your marketing ideas and insights in helping us position Acumen Management.

I have truly enjoyed speaking and sharing our insights

with thousands of individuals and working closely with many other independent consultants who have offered ideas and additional services to our clients. It has turned into a wonderful ride with so many benefits, mostly sharing my thoughts, ideas, tools, and systems with so many of our clients and seeing the positive impact on their organizations.

I need to thank Jeb Blount at Sales Gravy who came on board with the Sales Management Guru's focus on the toughest job in most organizations and is publishing our series of books.

Anne Stuart, my fabulous editor that had to work through all my ideas, broken sentences and created short, crisp ideas that will help sales organizations reach higher levels of achievement.

Lastly and most importantly, a huge thank you to my wife, Jolyne, who took the leap with me into this world of independence and uncertainty, while enduring many nights away from home and a seven day-a-week job focus. Her continuous faith and support has always been there for me.

I thank each of our clients for their support, encouragement and willingness to engage the Acumen philosophy of "building organizations through the execution of strategic sales management."

Ken Thoreson, President
Acumen Management Group Ltd.
www.AcumenManagement.com
www.YourSalesManagementGuru.com

1 | GETTING STARTED

*I*s it not a disincentive to strive for high levels of conversion and/or customer retention if you know you will be compensated in the same manner as an individual who fails to hit his or her numbers? If achievement entails no reward, not including those who receive intrinsic rewards for sales achievement, what reason would there be for trying?"
                                                    --Mark R. Platzer

Objective

Effective sales compensation plans play an important role in a company's overall sales strategy. At the same time, creating and implementing such plans can be challenging and frustrating. And it's important to keep in mind that the compensation plan is just one part of a comprehensive sales strategy designed to help the organization achieve its stated goals.

This book is intended to assist sales leaders in clearly planning, accurately developing, effectively implementing, wisely rolling out and closely monitoring their sales compensation plans.

I have designed this book to be an interactive and practical experience. As you work through it, you'll actually begin developing a compensation plan that will benefit you and your organization.

Planning and Research

The obvious first question is: "Where do I begin?" The answer: with the right mindset. An ideal approach for any large project is to *plan your work and work your plan.* In the case of compensation planning, your job starts with understanding important background information about your company, your sales team and the competitive environment that influences actions and results.

First, you need to understand both your company's strategic business and financial goals, both for the current fiscal year and for the long haul. This step will also help pinpoint the behaviors and results you want to achieve and kickstart your thinking about developing compensation plan that reflects those goals.

Address the following four questions:

1. Identify the company goals and objectives for the next 12-18 months, including:
   - Revenue objectives $ _____
   - Margin/profit objectives $ _____
   - Bookings/sales objectives $ _____
   - Unit sales targets (by area/practice) $_____
   - New product/service offerings $ _____
   - New product/service launch goals $ _____
   - Market-share growth objectives $ _____
   - Key account-retention objectives $ _____
   - New product/service launch goal $ _____

2. How did the company's performance during the past fiscal year compare to the established objectives? _____

   _____

   _____

   _____

3. What is the company's current cost of sales (CoS) as a percentage of sales or gross margin? _____%

4. Is there an objective to improve CoS, or is the company interested in acquiring net new customers *now*, at any cost?

   _____

   _____

Now analyze your existing compensation program by completing the following evaluation.

Sales Compensation Assessment

Rate your existing sales-compensation program by circling the answers to the following questions (1 = low; 5 = high).

1. How well do the existing plans basic components work?
   1 2 3 4 5

2. How well, as a percentage of quota achievement, is your existing plan working? 1 2 3 4 5

3. How well does the current plan represent the company's goals? 1 2 3 4 5

4. What percent of your sales team exceed last year's quota?
    (5=100%, 3=50%, 1=10%   1 2 3 4 5

5.   Overall, was your CoS within company guidelines?
    (5=100%, 3=within 15%, 1=not close)   1 2 3 4 5

6. How well does your compensation plan reflect industry
    standards?   1 2 3 4 5

7. How well did your sales team exceed the company's sales
    goals in the past year?   1 2 3 4 5

8. How well did your sales contests work in achieving their
    goals in comparison to their costs?   1 2 3 4 5

9. How well does the current compensation plan result in
    attaining the desired sales activities?   1 2 3 4 5

10. How well did the compensation plan accelerate revenues
    or margins to exceed your objectives?   1 2 3 4 5

Total Score: _____

- If your total score is greater than 40, you need few or no
  changes.
- If your total score is 21-39, I suggest making a change in
  one or two of the components of the plan—for instance,
  offering bonus percentage for net new customers, or setting a margin dollar or percentage goal objective.
- If your total score is less than 20, I suggest making major
  component changes. Focus on the areas with the lowest
  scores.
- **Guru Tip:** In reviewing your scoring, evaluate whether
  one or two answers may have over-weighted the results;
  if so, correct for those specific areas.

Further Compensation Plan Analysis

1. Does the plan need to better recognize the organization's long-term or short-term goals? _____
   _____

2. Identify the top three sales and corporate goals for next year. Guru Tip: if any of these goals can be impacted by sales compensation, be sure you include those objectives in your compensation plans, along with metrics for measuring success.

   a. _____
   b. _____
   c. _____

3. Should you consider a six-month focus rather than an annual sales compensation plan? **Guru Tip:** In a high-growth or turnaround situations, a six-month plan may be a more desirable strategic option. Good idea? Y/N

4. Identify three changes in your market, industry or company that are likely to occur in the next two years. Examples: government regulations, mergers, new offices, major product releases. **Guru Tip:** If these changes could impact earnings, revenues or compensation plans, make the pertinent changes in your compensation plan.

   a. _____
   b. _____
   c. _____

Company Goal Review and Analysis

1. Define the company's specific sales goals for the past year and the next 24 months (for instance, revenue/margin dollars, market-share percentage, growth percentage quarter over quarter, number of net new customer growth).

    _____

    _____

    _____

    _____

2. Answer the following questions: Does your sales organization consist of hunters or farmers? Does your sales team drive orders from all net new customers or selling to existing customers? Or is your team focused on long-term customer relationships, working in a "route" mentality or customer-service focus? Describe the specifics of the sales relationship.

    _____

    _____

    _____

3. Now consider: What specific aspects of a sales compensation plan could be used to achieve each goal by salesperson type or responsibility?

    _____

    _____

    _____

    _____

4. Define the activities that you desire for your sales team. Guru Tip: Consider which sales activities to measure in relation to exceeding your sales goals. For example, a goal of attaining net new clients requires focusing on making more net new sales calls and perhaps considering additional compensation for sales to net new clients.

_____

_____

_____

_____

5. Define the CoS equation. In calculating your CoS, do you include salary, commission at 100% of quota, organizational overhead, insurance costs, cell phone/wireless costs, marketing allocations and employer tax costs as well as product and service costs? There's no specific formula for this step; many organizations will use any combination of the above items to determine CoS. However, the management team must be in agreement with whatever formula you ultimately use. List the CoS components.

_____

_____

_____

_____

6. Define whether your company is at an early stage, a high-growth phase or at a mature level. **Guru Tip:** This is especially important to know. CoS will be higher in early-stage companies as compared to a more mature organizations because of increased go-to-market costs, new product launches or opening new offices or territories.

_____

_____

_____

7. Consider whether you have major new product or service launches planned for the next revenue period. <u>Guru Tip:</u> This may be important in two cases: first, if a large percentage of your existing customers will upgrade automatically or with little direct sales effort, and second, if a major new product or service launch represents a top company priority requiring a focused direct sales effort. In the first situation, it may not be necessary to pay a normal/full commission rate. In the second, you may consider paying a bonus commission based upon achieving a targeted level of new product or service acceptance.

_____

_____

_____

_____

8. Consider whether you have multiple products or services to be managed via a compensation plan. <u>Guru Tip:</u> Some organizations offer different levels of commission percentages and even different plans based on different product categories, margins or service-delivery models. These plans may be based upon margins and the organization's desire, need or competitive positioning to sell the product or service.

_____

_____

_____

_____

9. Consider any seasonal business or product issues. Are some of your offerings targeted so that they must be purchased or sold during certain time periods? <u>Guru Tip:</u> You may want to over-weight your plan for those periods. If customers simply drive demand–that is, if

they need to purchase at certain times -- then you may simply lower commissions for those products because of the lack of real sales efforts. If your marketing campaigns drive product acceptance rather than sales efforts or customer demands, then CoS must take into consideration that expense and lack of direct sales efforts.

_____

_____

_____

_____

10. Finally, take a close look at whether the existing compensation plan attracts the type of salespeople you want. If you are in the need of attracting hunters, or the need to build a client base in new markets your compensation plan must be designed to find and attract those individuals. These plans would include "good" salaries—but also much higher personal commission/compensation potential opportunity plans or if your business model has changed and you currently need long-term client relationships with lower margins, then you may expect higher salaries with lower overall CoS and total compensation values.

_____

_____

_____

_____

The Guru's team believes that prior to creating a sales compensation plan, you must simply consider your corporate business objectives, product/service requirements and the types of salespeople required to achieve those objectives. We like to suggest you need to *"align the soul of the individual with the goals of the organization."*

Review Sales Team Status

Once you understand the company's goals and business objectives and you've assessed your current plan, you should review your entire team's status to determine how and where to focus your sales management program. Following are four steps for undertaking this analysis:

1. Decide which activities and performance levels (quotas) the entire team must meet to achieve the company objectives. The most common target needing to be covered is the team sales and margin quota (with enough assigned to be equal to or greater than the team objective). **Guru Tip:** It's especially important to recognize that sales quotas must be substantially higher than the budget the management team requires to run the company.

There are three kinds of budgets:

- Bank budget or quota. This is the lowest acceptable number.
- Management budget or quota. This is the company management team's acceptable number to achieve its pre-defined objectives and where its budget/compensation targets are set.
- Sales budget or quota. This number must be set above the management number simply because it's not realistic to expect that all salespeople will achieve their individual quotas.

2. Next, break down the quota by individual sales position -- without names attached to ensure objectivity. **Guru Tip:** If you have assigned territories, consider whether the market is new, underdeveloped, lower-potential or

mature. Do you have a quota quotient based upon an industry-accepted demographic? For example, Microsoft knows the number of PCs owned per ZIP code and correlates potential software sales based on that number.

3. Next, insert team members' names, based on seniority, skill level, territory values and similar factors.

4. Once you've completed the assessment, review and list areas of sales strengths and areas requiring additional attention. Examples: A certain territory might include the same area as the corporate office, while another could be closer to the distribution center. More remote territories may require frequent driving or flying to ensure market coverage.

    Guru Tip: Consider scheduling a brainstorming session with your management-team members to discuss your team's sales positions, responsibilities, assignments, market conditions, industry competition and expectations. This meeting will offer you multiple points of view and help everyone understand the sales organization's requirements from marketing, product or service development sales support and CoS perspectives. This feedback will also be useful in planning your compensation introduction and rollout.

The sales compensation plan will provide additional focus for your salespeople, individually and as a team. It offers the most direct way to lead and motivate salespeople and to guide their activities. Most salespeople are success-motivated as well as income-motivated—they appreciate recognition for success by the company's leadership team and their peers. While compensation isn't the No.1 factor that most successful salespeople consider in accepting employment, it certainly ranks in the top five. (See "The Sales Management Guru's Guide to Hiring High-Performance Sales Teams" for advice on hiring the best, not just the best available.)

As noted earlier, it's also important to review your sales team's skills and levels of knowledge. Use the following list of questions as a guide for identifying the skill sets you need for a successful high-performance team and to assist you in judging their abilities to achieve the desired objectives or outcomes in the compensation plan you're developing.

Identifying Team Skill Sets

1. Are the sales teams' job activities currently focused on tasks that improve your chances of achieving the company's desired goals? Does the current compensation plan reinforce those activities? Does your sales-management system track and manage those activities? Can a compensation plan impact those activities?

   _____

   _____

   _____

   _____

   _____

2. How well are salespeople performing in areas such as total sales volume, sales to net new accounts or sales of particular items in the product or service category?

   _____

   _____

   _____

3. If you could instantly *change* any current skills or job activities represented on your sales team, what would you change? Can compensation impact their focus? <u>Guru Tip:</u> If you identify any, create a plan to train and address them.

_____

_____

_____

_____

_____

4. If you could *retain* any current skills or job activities of the sales team, what would you retain? Does your training plan or compensation plan reinforce those skills?

_____

_____

_____

_____

_____

<u>Guru Tip</u>: You can obtain additional insights from post-mortem contract analysis, won/lost analysis, sales management reviews and performance evaluations — as well as by simply asking questions of your sales teams, your new clients and your lost prospects. (Acumen's Interactive Sales Manager's Tool Kit includes a Won/Lost Report; it's available at www. AcumenManagement.com)

Means vs. Results

At this point, it's important to note that 99 percent of all sales compensation plans address results only (or ends). For example, the company will pay the salesperson 15 percent of all sales, or pay the manager 2 percent for every dollar sold. These plans don't include any important tactical efforts (or means) needed to accomplish the results. Here's an example of what's meant by tactical means: The salesperson will earn a bonus if X number of net new customers are signed each quarter.

Of course, results need to be a significant part of your sales compensation plan, but there are many ways to document and address other parts of behavior you are attempting to influence. (For more information, see Chapter 5, "One-to-One Tools for Driving Successful Results.")

Still, consider a combination of objectives based on results and proven important tactical actions or "means" before building your sales compensation plan. One caveat: This approach can be more difficult and time-consuming to measure than other approaches. If you choose this route, you must have excellent knowledge of the company's sales process and what actions it takes to be successful. A bonus dollar value could be paid on a quarterly basis or as "points earned" towards a yearly sales contest trip where additional incentives could be achieved, such as extra hotel nights. You must also consider the ability to physically track the information and salespeople's focus and capability to drive the desired end results without improperly reporting the data.

The following are several examples of means-oriented components for your sales compensation plan:

- **Pipeline:** A salesperson must have X times the dollar value of his or her quarterly quota in customer-delivered proposals that are less than 60 days old.

  Guru Tip: You'll need to know your close ratio of proposals delivered to the number of proposals won by salesperson and your entire team. It's important to closely inspect quality as well as simply tracking quantity. The Guru's team normally recommend three times quota for pipeline levels.

- **Proposals to new accounts:** A salesperson will receive a bonus or incentive for delivering proposals targeted to a particular job title, such as CIO, CFO or vice president of marketing, in four new accounts each quarter. Understanding probability of success and the need to increase your corporate visibility per account will be the most valuable determination of this metric.

- **Number of demonstrations or executive presentations per month:** This activity normally is a leading indicator of proposals and future business: Example: For every five demonstrations, a salesperson receives a bonus of, say, $250 — and there's no limit on the number of bonuses any one salesperson can win. Knowing the ratio of demos to sales will be helpful here. **Guru Tip:** It's important to clarify the definitions or rules regarding which actions qualify as a quality demonstration or presentation. These may include the attendees' titles or sales stage of the prospect.

- **Balanced product portfolio:** Here's an example: When one product or 100 percent of quota is achieved from each product portfolio category each month or quarter, the salesperson will increase his or her percentage of commission per sale from 3 to 4 percent. **Guru Tip**: Some companies require 100-percent quota attainment in each product category to qualify for the annual sales quota and sales trip.

Example: There may be four product categories, with two of great importance to the company and two of much lesser margin or vendor focus. However, those latter two categories may be products or services that act as leaders into much higher margin and value future sales. This is why it's crucial to ensure that your sales team and sales management are focused on achieving certain quota requirements for each product portfolio. It's equally important to understand the ideal salesperson's profile and how your sales compensation plan can help attract top people. Salespeople who pursue new accounts tend to be more aggressive and interested in higher-risk, higher-reward plans.

On the other side of the equation, sales executives responsible for managing existing customer accounts prefer compensation plans with a higher guaranteed salary component and lower commission component. (See "The Sales Management Guru's Guide to Hiring High-Performance Sales Teams" for more about finding, training and retaining high-powered salespeople.)

Keep in mind that not every plan must be based on hiring a single type of salesperson. Many mature organizations need both new account-oriented salespeople and installed-base customer-care salespeople. In those cases, sales leaders must design compensation plans that have enough flexibility to attract both types of candidates.

Positioning

Next, take a look at the company's product and service lifecycles and position in the marketplace, as well as the industry's maturity. Consider that market newcomers whose top goal is rapidly expanding the products and services they offer will view their sales compensation plans differently than mature market leaders in the same industry. Each situation requires different behaviors for success.

A targeted total sales strategy, complete with a properly designed sales compensation plan, is much more likely to succeed than a shotgun approach. Start by choosing the description that best fits your organization.

- **Your company has a high-revenue growth objective in a boom market with minimum competition.** If this is the situation, you may consider a six-month compensation plan that can be adjusted with a focus on growth percentage of quarter over quarter or past year over past year.

- **Your company needs to protect its customer base and maintain revenue growth objective in a mature market with many competitors**. You may consider organizational changes with inside customer account managers and outside sales teams, or you might create a compensation plan that encompasses current customer sales based on margin and net new customer compensation based upon revenue. You may also want to build a team compensation plan based upon several salespeople working together to achieve a territory sales objective.

- **Your company has a revenue and margin growth objective with a balanced product/service mix and stable, lower sales-intensity team.** Compensation planning should take into consideration achieving sales targets by product or service group with monthly margin goals and quarter-to-date revenue objectives. This would entail higher salesperson salaries and lower total commission earnings in relation to overall compensation. Customer satisfaction ratings might be considered as part of compensation.

- **Your company's goal is to maintain revenue and profit growth objective and increase focus on account conversion programs to a new product line.** In this case, compensation planning should consider a somewhat lower commission percentage on revenue and profit/margin based upon quota attainment with a ramped or accelerator commission percentages at 80 percent, 90 percent and 100 percent and above. A monthly bonus fee or additional percentage commission rates would be paid for all existing and net new account conversions, to the new product line.

- **Your company has a market leadership position and substantial new account objective and also believes that its top competitor is poorly servicing its customers.** Compensation plans may have lower commission levels and/or CoS because of the market leadership position plus a quarterly net new account revenue goals and quota number of net new customers added. Consider paying a bonus dollar value for all competitive replacements. Marketing would need to be coordinated to launch special competitive replacement packages and campaigns. These marketing costs should be considered in CoS calculations.

In each case, of course, the sales strategy, marketing and sales compensation plans would need to be coordinated. In most cases, you would want to consider sales training and customer service programs as well.

Compare the current fiscal year plan and its effectiveness to next fiscal year's goals to help construct your new plan. It may make sense not to change the components of your plan dramatically, instead maintaining the effective components from last year's plan as a basis for this year's plan. If your strategic objectives or market dynamics haven't changed significantly, your compensation plans may not need to be altered, either.

Dramatic change requires substantial time and effort up front to explain the reasons for change and the desired results. This type of change is in line with large movements in the industry or company strategy. **Guru Tip**: If major changes will occur, be sure to plan for ramping up your sales recruiting plan accordingly — and be aware that you may experience some attrition. (For more information on this issue, purchase "The Sales Management Guru's Guide to Hiring High-Performance Sales Teams.")

If the sales compensation plan evolves and improves, your team will focus achieving the objectives rather than just "beating" the plan. Many companies maintain a large chunk of their current plans from successful years, adding subtle changes based on new objectives.

In addition, avoid requiring salespeople to do too many things at once. When you tie rewards to multiple aspects of performance, it diffuses the salesperson's motivation to improve dramatically in any one area. Consequently, most successful compensation and incentive plans link rewards to no more than three job-performance factors. Those factors should be linked to the company's highest-priority sales and marketing objectives.

Salary? Commission? Bonus?

Determine the total target income levels you are willing to pay your sales team, including the percentage of base salary and the percentage of commission or bonuses. The decision about whether to offer average total pay or premium compensation depends on company size, positioning, name recognition in the industry and overall sales strategy.

This isn't to say that you should create sales earning limits or maximum earning potential. I believe in developing a philosophy on compensation around payment for performance, meaning simply that higher performers deserve higher levels of income and lower performers deserve lower levels. High-performing salespeople will be attracted to a sales culture built on recognition and sales compensation plans that reflect their desire to succeed.

In general, large well-established companies with large sales forces and good reputations in their industries tend to offer higher salaries with middle-of-the-road target income opportunities and higher levels of security. In addition, these companies typically offer established sales training programs, clear paths into management and advertising and marketing support for their products or services.

Smaller companies that haven't invested heavily in extensive marketing and training programs will compensate salespeople and sales management with higher target income opportunities based on a results-oriented larger commission component. Consequently, they must offer above-average compensation to attract experienced sales reps from other companies.

The percentage of salary versus commission/bonus also varies greatly. If the market is tight, higher salaries for proven professionals usually become the norm. Keep in mind that higher risk (lower salary) equals higher rewards (total compensation), while lower risk (higher salary) equals lower rewards (lower total compensation).

No matter how you design your plan, the issue of over-paying or underpaying the sales force is likely to come up. Overpayment can cause resentment and low morale among the companies other employees and managers. In determining incentive pay, it's important to consider the impact to overall employee morale and company philosophies.

On the other hand, underpaying salespeople can, at first glance, seem like a convenient way to hold down sales costs and enhance short-term profits. Don't be fooled. Every employee is important to your business and should be compensated accordingly, based upon the organization's objectives.

Still, of course, a consistent growth-oriented approach to sales is the key to your company's long-term success. So when in doubt, construct a results-oriented sales compensation plan that errs on the side of overpaying the best sales executives — the ones who achieve their objectives year after year.

Guru Tip: Recognize that once salespeople achieve their yearly break-even ratios, their contributions to your net profit increases, which in turn allows for dramatically accelerating commission rates.

One cautionary note: Even the best-designed sales compensation plan can become less effective over time due to changes in both the marketplace and the sales force. For that reason, many companies now review their compensation and incentive policies at least once every six months, making changes as needed.

Finally, a compensation plan should be presented with the overall employee benefits package, including profit-sharing, stock options, insurance, sale contests and company-sponsored plans.

Critical Things to Remember

- Complete all necessary organizational background work before you start constructing a compensation plan. The most important item to know: the company's goals and objectives for the fiscal year.

- Plan your work and work your plan! Lay out the steps necessary to construct an effective compensation plan, then make it happen.

- This point can't be over-emphasized: Compensation is just one facet of a total sales strategy. Don't be lulled into believing that the amount that you pay your sales executives will be the only ticket to achieving your bookings, sales and margin objectives. Without a comprehensive business strategy, sales leadership, marketing and attention to building a culture, your chances of success dwindle.

- A well-rounded compensation plan that rewards good performance on items that represent the means (that is, the pipeline) and the ends you desire (that is, high-margin sales) will become more and more effective. But also keep in mind that managing a plan with components built around the means will also be more time-consuming than other types of plans.

- Use the existing plan as a basis for next year's compensation plan. If the current plan has merit, the transition will be easier, meaning that sales executives will focus on selling rather than on trying to figure out the new plan and creating dissent.

- Before building the compensation plan, determine the total and target income levels you are willing to pay your sales executives, including the percentage representing base salary and the percentage for commission or bonuses.

- Consider reviewing your compensation and incentive plans every six months, adjusting as necessary to accommodate market, company, economic, product, service or business changes.

Activity 1: Analyzing a Compensation Plan

To complete this activity, think about the sales compensation plan(s) currently in place in your own organization. Answer the following questions:

1. Describe the plan(s). Is there more than one version being used? If so, why? Do you have different divisions? What are the various plans based on: Profit? Product? Sales?

2. Is the plan easy to understand? Are sales executives able to accurately calculate their own income on a monthly basis?

3. Does the plan(s) include personal or team incentives? Describe them.

4. Are the incentives designed to motivate sales staff to achieve the company's goals?

5. Does the plan allow your organization to meet its financial goals? Discuss.

6. Could the current plan(s) be improved in any way? How?

7. Is the plan attractive to top performers?

2 | DETERMINING METRICS FOR AN EFFECTIVE COMPENSATION PLAN

Calculating accurate cost of sales (CoS) is an important step in establishing justification for the sales compensation plan.

First, let's define CoS. Essentially, this is a measurement of the costs required to generate sales, revenue and/or profit. The most important aspect of determining your CoS is to understand which of your company's expenses should be considered sales expenses. Your internal financial person responsible for budget planning can identify these costs and confirm with you the margin generated per account or per product category. In some situations, companies may only use the cost of the product and commissions paid; in others, organizations may include these costs as well as the costs associated with marketing, benefits, and company operations.

In addition, CoS should be included in planning discussions because it confirms the financial basis for your compensation plan and its relationship to the company's financial objectives. It's important to understand the cost of attaining the sale or new account and the long-term (or lifetime value) profit that could be generated from your customers. This analysis determines the short-term and long-term return on sales for each account and helps justify the sales executive's commission payout. This is called the "lifetime value ratio."

Lifetime value is normally calculated by determining the cost of the original sale of a client, the three- or five-year cost of supporting that client and revenue or margin generated from that client over that three- or five-year period. All clients should be reviewed to determine whether you are building a long term "wallet-share" or penetration level from your client base. Knowing lifetime value will help you determine your support costs and business philosophies.

I suggest that you attempt to determine the cost to attain a client, the cost to support the client and the total revenue/ margin attained over three or five years from each customer. This longer-term look will help you determine the overall profitability of your customers and your "wallet share" of their budgets. In addition, after conducting this analysis, you'll see whether you are earning a proper return from your current customers or whether you're over-servicing, not taking the opportunity to offer additional products/services or not actively focused on selling to your customer base.

Basic Financial Metrics

To understand what's working and what needs improvement, you must establish basic financial metrics. This step goes beyond simply answering the question of "Did I make my monthly quota?'" Performing a comparison between your organization's numbers and established financial metrics will help you evaluate your organization's strengths and weaknesses. That, in turn, will help you design and implement the components of an effective sales-compensation plan that not only works to achieve your objectives but is also cost effective.

The Guru has defined a few simple financial metrics that will help sales leaders build great and successful sales teams.

Break-even calculation by sales position. Your objective is to determine how much gross margin or revenue sales executives need to generate to pay for themselves. You should also have completed this calculation for your entire sales organization.

1. For each sales executive, calculate the costs of:
    +   Salary
    +   Benefits and General Overhead (**Guru Tip**: I usually multiply the salary times 30 percent for this number)
    +   Commission earnings at 100 percent of quota
    +   Annual car allowance
    +   Cell phone/wireless Internet allowance
    +   Annual travel/entertainment costs
    +   Computer costs
    +   Office overhead

2. Calculate the average margin percent per sale.

3. Divide the total costs per salesperson (#1) by the average margin percent per sale (#2) to determine the required sales to break even. Example:
    +   Salary of $45,000
    +   Benefits of 30 percent times salary = $13,500
    +   Commission at 100 percent = $30,000
    +   Monthly car allowance of $200 times 12 months = $2,400
    +   Cell phone/wireless Internet allowance (for this example, these costs have been included in overhead)

+ Travel/entertainment of (average per rep) $1,000 annually
+ Company-supplied PC costing $4,000
+ Office overhead average per employee of $5,000

Total Costs: $105,900

The total costs of $105,900 divided by the average margin percent per sale of 35 percent means that, to break even, you need $302,571 in sales or revenues from this salesperson.

Guru Tip: If you are using a ramped or accelerator commissions plan, your first break is on your break-even point. Once you move over the break point on a salesperson, your company's profitability jumps and you can afford a higher level of commission over that number.

For example: If you're using a quarterly payment commission plan and using the annual sales quotas, your first break point for commission rate would be $75,643 — taking the $302,571 annual break even-number from above and dividing by 4. (This assumes a flat revenue objective for each quarter).

An accelerated plan could look as follows*:

• 3 percent commissions paid on all sales up to the $75,763.

• 7 percent commissions paid between $75,764 and $100,000

• 12 percent on sales over $100,000

(*example purposes only)

Sales efficiency modeling and goal determination. The objective is to determine how much cost it takes to generate $1 of gross margin.

Calculate: Total sales team target for total sales costs divided by total gross margin at 100 percent of quota. The following example applies.

- Total gross margin to be generated at 100 percent of quota = $325,000
- Total team sales costs $250,000 divided by $325,000 = 77 percent
- Therefore, it takes 77 cents of cost to generate $1 of gross margin.

Let's put that in context. Generally,

- Less than 65 cents of cost to generate $1 of gross margin is **excellent**.
- Sixty-six to 80 cents of cost to generate $1 of margin is **very good**.
- Eighty-one to 90 cents of cost to generate $1 of gross margin is **good**.
- Ninety-one to ninety-nine cents of cost to generate $1 of gross margin is **okay**.
- More than $1 of cost to generate $1 of gross margin **needs improvement**.

The developmental or maturity stage of your company will determine your sales efficiency goal. Although early-stage companies are more apt to drive sales and customer installs, they will find it helpful to know their acquisition and maintenance costs for growing market share.

Sales productivity modeling and goal determination. Many organizations boast about their sales growth without discussing the cost to produce these numbers.

This financial metric allows you to set productivity goals that focus on growth in a more responsible manner. Adding substantially more cost (for example, three sales executives at $100,000 cost per sales executive) to gain an additional 10 percent in sales and margin will only work if there's a substantial lifetime value/profit for each customer account.

Don't get me wrong—to grow your business, you need to invest in your sales staff and bring on new members who typically are non-productive for the short term. The point here is that you shouldn't be fooled by sales growth only. Understand the fundamentals involved to gain a complete picture of your success so that you can replicate competent actions year after year.

The equation is simple. The number of sales executives divided by the total quota or sales and margin sold will provide a measure of true sales productivity. For example:

- Eight sales executives have a total annual sales quota of $9,565,000 or $1,195,625 per sales executive and $2,773,850 in annual gross margin, or $346,731 per sales executive.

- These eight sales executives achieved $10,235,000 in annual sales and $2,865,800 in annual gross margin or $1,279,375 per sales executive in sales and $358,225 in gross margin results.

- The team was 107 percent of the per-sales executive annual sales objective ($2,865,800 achieved divided by $1,195,625 quota) and 103 percent of the per sales executive annual gross margin objective ($358,225 achieved divided by $346,731 quota).

This brings us to two important conclusions: First, you can discuss total team effort and comparison in conjunction with individual success stories. Second, when establishing targets for next year, you can build them around team objectives and work down to individual targets. **Guru Tip**: If this is a new idea for you, calculate these ratios over the past three or four years to determine a trend review and set a standard series of ratios to use if your sales compensation plan has been designed to achieve those standards.

Critical Things to Remember

- Calculating accurate CoS is an important part of establishing justification for the sales compensation plan.

- The most important aspect of determining your CoS is to understand which specific expenses should be considered sales expenses.

- Basic financial metrics are easy to build. Just follow the examples and guidelines in this chapter and track your results quarter to quarter.

- Establishing and evaluating basic financial metrics can lead to fundamental insights that provide a complete picture of your success so that you're able to replicate competent actions year after year.

Activity 3: A Few Calculations

1. Given the following data, calculate the number required to break even.

Salary:	$ 65,000
Benefits:	35% of salary
Commission:	100%
Monthly car expense:	300
Travel expense per rep:	4,500
Average office expense per rep:	6,000
Average margin per sale:	40%
Sales break-even is: _____	

2. Given the following data, calculate the cost to generate $1 of gross margin:

Total annual sales expense budget = $ 250,000

Total gross margin to be generated = $ 325,000

Sales efficiency ratio: _____

Examples will vary based upon each sales organization.

Answers:

1. Sales break even (B/E): $246,500

2. Sales efficiency ratio: 77

Activity 4: Chapter 2 Benefit Statement
1. The most important concept I learned in Chapter 2 was: 2. My action steps will be:

3 | CHOOSING A TYPE OF SALES COMPENSATION PLAN

Before we examine the types of sales compensation plans, it's important to define several key terms.

A compensation plan is a package of employee benefits that may include a base salary, commission and/or bonus payments, medical and insurance options and expense reimbursement. Obviously, a solid compensation package must be competitive in the marketplace to attract and retain great sales executives. The costs of planned sales contests should also be considered when developing a compensation package.

The core ingredient of all sales compensation plans, except in 100 percent- commission situations, is salary. **Salary** is a fixed sum of money paid at regular intervals for performing prescribed work on the company's behalf. When sales executives receive salaries, they should be held accountable for performing specific tasks in exchange for those salaries. (I discuss a 100-percent commission plan later.)

Most sales organizations expect that, when they hire sales executives, those new employees will go through an on-boarding new employee training and introductory period during which no sales may be generated and, consequently, no commissions (when applicable) will be earned. If a straight commission plan is offered where no salary is paid, it's appropriate to offer the sales executive a **draw against future commissions** and/or **bonuses** for a limited period (usually three to six months, depending upon the length of the sales cycle). The draw amount is paid on a regular basis and can be used in a salary-plus- commission/bonus plan or in a 100-percent commission plan.

With a salary-based plan, there could be a draw that is in addition to the sales executive's salary. The combination of salary and draw provides a guaranteed, fixed income level until the sales executive becomes productive. In a 100-percent commission plan, the draw is typically paid monthly beginning with the start-up period, allowing the sales executive to generate a minimum level of income.

As a company, you can stipulate that the draw amount is either **recoverable** or **non-recoverable**. A *recoverable* draw means that the sales executive is responsible to repay the draw amount from future commissions and/or bonuses earned. *Non-recoverable* means that the draw amount doesn't have to be repaid; the company views the draw as an investment in helping sales executives meet their own financial obligations while undergoing training.

In a salary-plus-commission/bonus plan, the draw can be either recoverable or non-recoverable, based on the company's philosophy. In 100-percent commission plans, the draw is recoverable nearly every time because the program is based on a high-risk, high-return mentality I will discuss this concept more in the upcoming section on types of compensation plans).

Commission is payment based on the *direct, individual results* of successful activity by the sales executive. Typically, the company rewards results based upon a sales executive's volume in bookings, invoicing and/or margin. Commission payments usually occur soon after a sale is completed or an invoice has been paid (for example, within two weeks). Because there's a direct link between sales volume and amount of commission received, commission payments can be highly motivational in generating a strong sales effort.

Bonus incentives are another method designed to reward high levels of performance. They are specified dollar values based upon achievement. Bonus plans have two focus objectives: 1) individual achievements and 2) sales team achievements.

Team performance and results: Although bonuses can be paid to individuals, you maybe also rewarding the entire team's performance. For example, an objective for the entire company might be to raise customer satisfaction results by 2 percent. If measurements show customer satisfaction has moved 4 percentage points, a bonus of $5,000 might be split among all of the customer-service team members. **Guru Tip:** We recommend sales team compensation plans as well.

Individual performance and results: These types of bonus plans generally aren't paid immediately; instead, they are paid over longer periods of time. For example, if the compensation plan focused on net new customers, each sales executive might have a quarterly objective of signing up five new accounts per quarter. Each salesperson who achieves that number would receive a bonus of, say, $2,500.

Types of Compensation Plans

While there are different types of compensation plans within each industry, there are also different factors to consider in designing the right sales compensation plan for your company: the target market you are pursuing, the company's goals, salesperson experience and sales cycle time frame, to name a few.

The following table summarizes six types of compensation plans:

Plan Type	Risk vs. Return	Environment	Strengths	Weaknesses
Salary + bonus	Low risk/low return	Large base of accounts to maintain	Nurturing environment; stable, consistent image	Will not attract "hunters"; sales team can become stodgy
Salary + Commission	Medium Risk/Medium Return	Effective for most situations/ environments	Greatest Flexibility	Pays salary without results
100% Commission	High Risk/High Return	Not highly capitalized/ rewards results only	Pays only for results	Hard to attract experienced reps
Bookings/ Sales Only	Focuses on sales; disregards margin concerns	Growth environment; focus on winning customers now	Sales reps pursue every deal	Consider quality
Bookings/ sales plus margins	Need to close profitable deals vs. *win at any cost*			

Plan Type	Risk vs. Return	Environment	Strengths	Weak- nesses
Margins only	Need to focus on value-add opportunities			

Timing

One more consideration to review before designing the right sales compensation plan for your company: When do you pay the sales executive? There are many theories on the payment of commissions.

The most common option is to pay a certain percent of the total commission due when the contract is signed and a certain percent of the commission with the customer's final payment. You should consider how long the sales process takes and how many transactions or orders are sold per year. (**Guru Tip**: I like to include a down payment from the customer a t the time of order, if applicable.)

Other considerations in commission payment can be based upon invoice payment by the customer, which may help in cash flow management.

Or commissions may be paid on all invoiced values on a weekly or bi-weekly basis. Obviously, if payments are disputed or not paid, commissions will be charged back to the salesperson.

Because commission is a direct result of individual effort, payment should be made quickly, accurately and on time. No matter what the size of the organization, commission reconciliation and payments, process, systems and timing are critical to consider. Confusion about compensation and errors in computing it are two of the biggest frustrations that can demoralize a sales organization. They are also both major reasons why top performers tend to leave organizations.

Compensation plans must be easy to design, easy to understand, easy to calculate and easy to administer. If commissions are paid based upon invoice, then a monthly report showing each invoice and the corresponding commission rate and dollar value must be generated. Note that while some commission payments are usually connected to the receipt of customer payment, the invoice date value and payment must be included on the reconciliation statement. If commissions are based upon payment, you must consider the length of sale, delivery of the product or implementation of the service or level of salesperson involvement in the post-sales environment. For example, if the product or service requires a six-month implementation process, sales and the payment cycle are spread out over the six months and commissions maybe paid up front or at predefined specific checkpoints.

There are several theories about the best length for a compensation plan. Most companies develop a detailed yearly sales compensation plan that includes the sales budget and sales objectives. Typically, plans are 12 months long and include monthly or quarterly reviews. This isn't to say that all incentives or accelerators are based upon annual goals. In many situations, the compensation plan maybe defined for a 12-month cycle, but the plan may include monthly and quarterly objectives.

Another option is a six-month plan. Organizations in transition or turnaround mode and those positioned for high growth should consider shorter-term plans. A six-month plan allows managers to test their theories and adjust the plan based on results. This approach also helps protect salespeople from unjust or unrealistic programs or environments that limit their opportunity to earn the expected income levels.

Critical Things to Remember

- Most sales compensation plans have a draft, salary and commission and/or bonus component. Commission is designed to compensate individual performance and should be paid soon after the salesperson achieves the desired goal. Bonuses are designed to compensate team and individual longer-term efforts.

- A draw against future commissions/bonuses is designed to provide sales executives with guaranteed income levels until they are trained and self-sufficient. The draw can be recoverable or non-recoverable.

- When constructing a sales compensation plan, keep in mind that the general rule of thumb is higher risk (lower salary) should deliver higher rewards (total compensation) while lower risk (higher salary) delivers lower rewards.

- When a sales executive earns a commission or bonus payment, the reporting must be accurate and on time.

Activity 5: Design a Compensation Plan

Discuss the following situation:

You are the sales manager for a major information services organization. Your large sales staff includes:

1. Forty-eight marketing specialists in various divisions, who each have the responsibility to support and sell relevant services to an average of 2,500 customers.

2. Twenty-five key account representatives who are assigned to support either one large account or several smaller accounts grouped by industry.

What types(s) of compensation plan(s) would you design to meet the needs of these different sales teams? Describe your solutions.

Activity 6: Chapter 3 Benefit Statement

1. The most important concept I learned in Chapter 3 was:

2. My action steps will be:

4 | INCORPORATING INCENTIVE PROGRAMS

Sales contests are short or long-term incentive programs designed to motivate sales personnel to accomplish specific sales objectives in a specific time frame. They may or may not be addressed in the sales compensation plan. However, they must be considered in overall cost of sales when delivering a sales compensation plan. The most important aspect to consider is that any payments for sales contest or sales games are paid as a result of incremental revenues/margins over the management or sales budgets.

Sales leaders must first determine whether the contest will be profitable with the additional cost of incentives. Is the justification increased market share? Incremental new revenue? New product or service introduction? Or sales culture development?

The most common contests or games tend to be short-term, implemented at the last minute and designed to drive results quickly. In most cases, a nervous sales leadership team feels that extra motivation is required to achieve monthly or quarterly objectives. **<u>Guru Tip</u>**: Consider a more strategic approach. Plan sales contests at the beginning of the year with the organization's objectives in mind. These would include a yearly sales trip contest, quarterly events to spur the right activity and create a sense of fun for your team. This allows sales leaders to develop and budget for a yearly ongoing plan, seasonal activity programs and new product or service launch initiatives.

For example: In many cases, the fourth-quarter focus is on closing business to make the year-end results. As a result, depending upon the length of your sales cycle and product offering, the following first quarter lacks sufficient opportunities. **Guru Tip**: Consider having your plans include a contest centered on generating new leads in the fourth quarter to insure a strong pipeline of leads to start the first quarter strong. Consider a first quarter contest to both close business and generate new leads.

Before creating a contest, the sales leader must consider its potential impacts:

- Will the contest add incremental new business levels or simply shift future orders to a nearer term?
- Are all sales executives on an equal basis for the contest?
- Is the team anticipating a "contest-per-month" or "contest-per-quarter" mentality from the leadership team and, as a result, holding orders until the next contest hits?
- Are your clients/prospects expecting a "quarterly discount or promotion and will wait for your offer?
- Are you training our prospects and customers to wait for special promotions before purchasing?
- Is the contest compelling to the sales team?

With the answers to those questions in mind, here are a few insights for creating a successful contest.

Make sure the contest length equals the sales-cycle length.
By creating a sales contest that falls within the normal sales
cycle, the sales executive generates the lead, moves the account through the sales cycle and closes the opportunity in
line with the contest time frame. This allows for properly in-
centing the salesperson and/or customer for taking action.
Many sales organizations shorten contest time frames to generate short-term results. Taking that route is fine as long as
you understand that you're paying extra dollars for results
now as opposed to during the typical sales cycle. You may be
paying extra commissions simply to move orders/sales that
you would normally be gaining.

If building a solid pipeline is a 90-day process in your
sales organization, then assigning a lead-generation contest
for an entire quarter makes sense and allows the team to gear
up and creates new sales and activity results spurred on by
the contest. In another situation, offering a closing incentive
to early in the buying process will simply delay orders or
provide for lower discounts or gross margin valves.

Be purposeful! Explain the logic behind the contest and
tell the team what results you expect. Amazing things happen when you communicate expectations. Specific objectives
could be based upon:

- Increasing sales volumes
- Stimulating specific product/service sales
- Increasing market penetration
- Introducing new products or services
- Acquiring new clients
- Improving customer service
- Replacing competitive accounts
- Overcoming seasonal slumps
- Erasing unfavorable inventory levels

Guru Tip: Incorporate an exciting theme into your announcement — use something topical, geographical, historical, sports-related, etc. The key is making the contest fun and linking it to desired sales activities. Remember, you have to "sell" the contest to your team and build up their excitement around it. This kind of sales leadership will enhance and build on your desired culture.

For example: Assume each salesperson is a fictitious professional basketball player on a fictitious team. Selling Product A (based on a higher contract value) equals 3 points; selling Product B equals 2 points and selling Product C, D or E equals1 point (a free throw). Split the team into several groups; let each group pick a team name, mascot and slogan. There are two ways to win. In the first, the team with the most points wins and each team member earns a $500 shopping spree at a national chain-electronics store. In the second, the three players with the highest individual point totals receive $1,500, $1,000 and $500 respectively for the same shopping spree. Other ideas or themes:

- **Make Music!** Provide each salesperson with a kazoo. Have them learn a simple song; then roll out the contest. Winners receive $500 towards music or electronics purchases at a Best Buy store.

- **Put the Pedal to the Metal:** This one is based on the Indianapolis 500. Create a poster with cars racing around the track based upon each salesperson's sales performance. Arrange for a road trip to a NASCAR race, or even some go-kart racing to enhance the race environment.

- **Kentucky Derby:** Host a mint julep party and plan a weekend hotel getaway event for the contest winners. During the contest, hold a "horse race" showing each person and team as they progress around the track.

- **North vs. South:** Divide the team into two groups with team targets, based upon Civil War themes. Provide simple costumes for each team and report weekly on the battles fought and won.

- **"Wanted":** Create a competitive replacement game based on pictures of your competitors on posters. Pay $500 for each replacement.

Remember that any contest or promotion with a theme needs to be clearly planned and promoted. Attempt to kick off the contest in person so that everyone hears the message at the same time. Create a sense of excitement!

Once communicated, the results should be published consistently and in public so everyone knows where they stand. For example, place a large board, which tracks results in a public location or online using a SharePoint or other groupware tool. There should be no guessing required to know how each individual and/or team is progressing. Continual reinforcement is critical to keep everyone focused on the event. In addition, create a special environment when the winners are announced.

For instance, you might schedule a monthly sales luncheon, a monthly all employee meeting, a morning office breakfast with your sales and support teams, or possibly having your company president make the presentations. **Guru Tip**: During your regular company meetings, let everyone know about the progress of your sales contests.

Pay rewards promptly. There is nothing more de-motivating than the excitement of winning a contest being lost due to slow management-team follow-up.

Provide a contest that's fair—with a stretch. The Guru highly recommends that you not create a competition or content where everyone will win even if it results in only

75 percent attainment of quota. Avoid creating an environ-ment of entitlement. If the same person wins every contest, consider alternatives for better balancing the opportunities, such as team contests or competitions based on percentages of quota.

Mix individual and team opportunities to win. Consider pairing non-sales employees with sales team members to cre-ate a company-wide contest and encourage cooperative effort. The non-sales employees may be encouraged to find leads, share customer insights and encourage the salesperson.

Make rewards meaningful. Sales-contest experts believe that effective incentives must equal at least 4 percent of a sales executive's total compensation. If you can't afford this level of investment, add some sort of personal recognition, such as having the CEO take contest winners and their spouses or partners out to dinner. Try non-financial awards such as computers, professional sales tools or items that are person-ally important to salespeople.

Rewards should be gifts, not cash. People remember the gifts they won long after the contest ends. One sales execu-tive won a high-quality electric shaver that lasted 10 years. The idea was that every time he used the shaver, it would bring to mind the company and the positive experience of that sales contest. Consider offering clothing allowances, high-end watches, hotel weekends or sales tools such as com-puter cases or GPS units.

Include the family in the contest. Mail the contest over-view to the sales executive's home. Make sure numerous gifts are family-oriented, such as a trip to Disney World or a family cruise. **Guru Tip**: Consider including a stipulation such as: At 100 percent of quota the spouse will go on the trip; at 110 percent the salesperson will be invited.

Coordinate internal incentive programs with customer promotions. If a sales executive earns points towards a trip for selling Product A, then customers also have an incentive—say, earning 20 percent off of Product A if purchased during the same period. This creates motivation for both parties to move forward now rather than later. If the sales executive is aware of the contest and the customer isn't, its effectiveness is lessened considerably.

Never end the sales contest on the last day of the month or sales period. Instead, conclude it five days before the end date. If the contest ends the last day of the month, last-minute problems can pop up to interfere with the program's success, such as customer vacations, illnesses or missed appointments. Setting an earlier deadline ensures that orders and sales will be completed and recorded before the end of the month. Setting an earlier deadline makes the sales manager's life easier and it also allows you five days to make up the difference or push for additional sales.

Put the rules in writing and make sure everyone understands them. When the rules are fuzzy and the contest announcement lacks examples of what's needed to win, chaos results. Questions will probably still come up; when they do, the sales leader should address them clearly and in writing. Without clearly defined rules, top performers will become disillusioned and the entire team could lose enthusiasm for current and future promotional programs.

Critical Things to Remember

- Sales contests are short or long-term incentive programs designed to motivate sales personnel to accomplish specific objectives in a set time frame or address other issues not covered in the compensation plan.

- A good rule of thumb to ensure effectiveness: Offer a contest payout that's at least 4 percent of the executive's salary.

- Gifts, rather than cash payouts, can create long-lasting goodwill.

- Keep everyone updated on the contest progress. When it's over, publicly acknowledge winners and results.

Activity 7: Design a Sales Contest

Create a fictitious company with fictitious products and company objectives. (One example: a bicycle retailer seeking to stabilize seasonal sales fluctuations.) Design a sales contest for this company's sales representatives.

1. Define the contest strategy and rules.

2. Define the criteria for winning the contest.

3. Cost justify the contest to your management

4. Determine what prizes will be offered?

5. Present your contest plan to the group.

Activity 8: Chapter 4 Benefit Statement
1. The most important concept I learned in Chapter 4 was:
2. My action steps will be:

5 | ONE-TO-ONE TOOLS FOR DRIVING SUCCESSFUL RESULTS

As noted earlier, an effective sales compensation plan is one component for establishing a thorough company sales strategy. The following tools are designed to complement the sales compensation plan and provide a complete package of expectations and measurement tools that are simple and focused on the results needed to be successful.

The Goal Sheet

This tool allows the sales manager and salespeople to develop the Five Key Responsibilities Areas (KRAs) for success. It's used monthly, quarterly and annually for performance reviews. (For a sample goal sheet, see Appendix E.)

I'm discussing the goal sheet here because it's directly related to the sales compensation plan, as well as to another tool that we'll discuss later in this chapter: the job-description document. Although the goal sheet and sales compensation plan may have some identical objectives, they may also be quite different. Sales compensation plans are results-oriented and standardized to meet company criteria. Goal sheets contain a combination of means and results customized for each sales executive.

An employee who accomplishes all goals at the **fully achieving level** will have very good results for the year. An employee who accomplishes all goals at the **overachieving level**
will have an outstanding year.

KRAs represent the three to five areas that are most important for an individual's success. Identifying the KRAs
from among the hundreds of tasks an employee pursues each
year helps direct the focus to the goals with the greatest bang
per buck.

**Sales managers and sales executives must jointly iden-
tify goals and KRAs.** The following goal sheet format is
designed to be simple and convenient to complete for both
parties.

Goals: Establish three to five goals and list them in order of
importance.

Objective: Start each objective with the word "achieve," and
state the goal for clarity (for instance: "Achieve annual sales
and margin objective of $1.5 sales million and $600,000 of
margin attainment."

Weight: You have a total of 100 percent to work with for
all goals combined. The greater the weight assigned to each
goal, the greater its importance for both the individual and
the team. Typically, **sales and margin quota achievement** is
the No. 1 goal with the highest weight.

There's also a 100 percent weight for each individual
goal. Sometimes you'll have two parts within a single goal
(an "a" and "b"). This helps you divide the goal into components when applicable. For example: "Achieve annual sales
and margin quota objective" includes two parts that work

hand-in-hand and are listed as a single goal in KRA No. 1. Still, you'll want to measure the critical components separately and split the overall goal into two pieces.

Measurement criteria: What exactly is the sales executive responsible for in achieving the goal? This part is critical. Be specific and detailed in describing the expectations. Every objective should be both specific and measurable. For example: "Achieve annual sales and margin quota objective" is the goal stated for KRA #1. There should be no misunderstandings or ambiguity about what's expected.

Next, describe the actual measurement criteria for *fully achieving* and *overachieving*. Fully achieving refers to the numeric and/or alpha measurement level your company sets for accomplishing this objective. The sales manager should not be making subjective decisions here; the measurement should be consistent for the entire team. Some organizations use a range of 90 to 104 percent, which indicates that 90 percent is the minimum acceptable level for fully achieving all objectives. In other cases, 100 percent flat is the measurement level. You'll need to set your own levels for success.

Overachieving refers to the company's "stretch" goals. These goals are for sales executives who achieve what's expected and seek additional challenges. These goals should, of course, be higher than the fully achieving level.

Goal Sheet Implementation

The sales manager constructs the initial goal sheet based on the company's strategic objectives and individual departmental goals and requirements. For a sheet with the recommended maximum of five goals:

- **Three goals** should represent standard procedure for all sales executives (for example, achieving sales and margin quotas).

- **One goal** should be personally designed to help the sales executive work on an area needing improvement (for example, securing 80 percent of customers to long-term service agreements).

- **One goal** should be targeted to the entire team (for example, achieving an overall customer-attrition rate of less than 5 percent).

The goals will tie into the sales compensation plan — but they don't have to be precisely aligned. The goal sheet is a combination of tactics and means (that is, the sales pipeline) necessary to accomplish important goals plus results, or ends (that is sales and margin quotas). Because the sales compensation plan is typically based and paid upon results only, the goal sheet, with its focus on means and results, offers a handy way for sales managers to focus their teams.

How involved should sales executives be in setting their own goals? The answer depends on each person's seniority and track record. **Guru Tip**: The sales leader should approve all goals and ensure that the ratios are accurate, provide a stretch objective and make sure they are realistic for each salesperson.

For a new sales executive with no proven success, the manager may simply set the objectives with very little discussion. But for sales executives who are mature, self-motivated and successful, the manager should take a more consultative approach to finalizing the goal sheet — always keeping the company's objectives in mind along with the being aware of the individual's personal goals This is has been described as aligning the goals of the corporation with the soul of the individuals.

The Job Description

Now let's bring the job description into the mix.

The job description is more comprehensive than the five KRAs and sales compensation components. This is your chance, in a simple and efficient format, to completely and thoroughly describe the roles, responsibilities and expectations for a successful sales executive. (See Appendix B for an example.)

The first section addresses a sales executive's role in your company, ideally defining the job in five or fewer lines. The second section deals with job responsibilities; the third includes the five KRAs from the goal sheet. (For more on job descriptions, see "The Sales Management Guru's Guide to Hiring High-Performance Sales Teams.")

Together, these three tools — the sales-compensation plan, the goal sheet and the job description — form a pyramid for success. The job description forms the base of the pyramid, the goal sheet is in the middle and the compensation plan is at the top.

Delivering the Tools

At the start of each fiscal year, the sales manager should schedule one-on-one sessions with each sales executive. The sales manager should use all three tools to establish expectations for a successful year.

After that initial meeting, the sales manager should schedule one-on-one reviews either monthly or quarterly, with a final review at the end of the six- or 12-month period. (For a sample Salesperson Development Plan, see Acumen's Interactive Sales Manager's Tool Kit, available at www. AcumenManagement.com). The sales manager should also meet privately with each salesperson once each month or quarter to review their goal sheets and track their progress. For the six-month and year-end reviews, the sales manager should expect longer discussions—about 60 to 75 minutes each—and those conversations should be documented. (For more on coaching and mentoring, read "The Sales Management Guru's Guide to Leading High-Performance Sales Teams.")

All one-on-one sessions between the sales manager and individual sales executives should be viewed as "quality time," giving them a chance to talk without interruption. The sales manager should not only discuss each person's results, but also share their ideas, suggest tactics and provide guidance for continued success. Reviews are the sales managers' time to create trust and confidence with their teams. Successful sales executives will not find such sessions threatening; they thrive on receiving feedback.

Critical Things to Remember

- A goal sheet with three to five objectives will focus your sales executives on individual achievement and team success.

- The goal sheet and sales compensation plan work hand-in-hand, but don't require identical measuring capability.

- The job description is the base component of the sales-success pyramid (which also includes the compensation plan and the goals sheet). The descriptions should cover everything that sales executives need to know about their jobs and what's expected of them.

- Sales managers should schedule consistent monthly or quarterly sessions to review goal sheets with individual salespeople.

- Keep all plans and documents simple. By delivering all three tools together, you're ensuring that sales executives know what's expected of them every day — and the sales manager can discuss results with them as needed.

Activity 9: Write a Job Description

Because the job description, with its great attention to detail, provides the base of the sales-success pyramid, try writing a description for your current job. Begin with a title and a short description of the position. Identify the main responsibility categories and then define required tasks. Here's an example:

Job Title: Sales Executive
Position Description: Responsible for meeting the needs of a target market, establishing long- term relationships and selling products and services to meet the organization's financial goals.

A. Prospect for Customers
1. Identify territory boundaries
2. Identify potential customers
3. Qualify customers
4. Etc.

B. Sell Products/Services
1. Establish relationship/build trust
2. Identify customer needs
3. Provide solutions/make recommendations
4. Etc.

Once you've created the job description, try your hand at creating a goal sheet.

Activity 10: Chapter 5 Benefit Statement
1. The most important concept I learned in Chapter 5 was:
2. My action steps will be:

6 | FIVE STEPS TO BUILDING A COMPENSATION PLAN

Now let's talk about building your company's sales compensation plan. Constructing an effective compensation plan involves using a step-by-step plan to make sure you cover all the bases. In this chapter, you'll find a proven model that's worked for many organizations.

Step 1: Start with research.

Effective sales compensation plans aren't devised overnight. They evolve over time, changing based on the organization's needs. So start the process by evaluating the results of the current or previous year's plans — good, bad and inconsequential. <u>Guru Tip</u>: If you plan to announce a new compensation plan in January, begin your review in October. Then consider these questions:

- **Goals:** Did the company achieve its goals and objectives for the fiscal year? Did the sales team achieve its goals? By halfway through the year, did you feel that the compensation plan objectives were in line with the company's goals and objectives? <u>Guru Tip</u>: As mentioned previously, some organizations run six-month compensation plans. Shorter-term plans may be ideal in extremely fast-growth companies or in organizations in tough, challenging turnaround situations.

- **Target incomes:** Are the target incomes for the sales organization competitive with the marketplace? Are top sales people are adequately rewarded?

- **Competitiveness:** Is the current sales-compensation plan competitive with the market? Are you finding it difficult to attract experienced salespeople? Have you lost salespeople to competitors or other companies? Are compensation concerns a recurrent theme of your exit interviews? **Guru Tip**: To validate your compensation plans, consider contacting industry associations that may have undertaken compensation studies or industry consultants who understand compensation planning.

To answer the first question, you will need to meet with the company's senior management team to review and evaluate the goals and results. For the last two questions, your company's human-resources director and your industry associations may have industry compensation data for comparison.

Finally, identify in writing what went right and what's working well, as well as which areas need improvement or additional attention. This provides a foundation for constructing next year's plan.

Step 2: Create an outline.

Next, sit down with the senior management team to identify or review company goals and objectives. (**Guru Tip**: You may also wish to use the Compensation Plan Assessment Tool in Appendix A for this exercise.) This discussion should cover:

- Company strategic business objectives
- Sales and margin growth targets
- Quotas for the sales leader
- Quotas for each sales position
- CoS targets
- New account growth objectives
- Customer retention targets
- Target income at 100 percent achievement of all sales objectives per sales position
- Sales efficiency and sales productivity objectives (see Step 3 for more details).

After aligning company goals with all departmental targets, you can discuss numerous compensation methods and scenarios for achieving the established fiscal-year goals.

Example: One corporate goal is to add 20 net new customers each quarter in this fiscal year. The company will pay an additional bonus for each new customer. The applicable compensation component could be developed at a later stage to read like one of the following two options.

- **Option 1:** "Every **net new** account sold will result in a one-time bonus of $500 paid added to your standard earned commission and paid within two weeks of the contract signature." If this were a valid plan, you would want to make sure there's a written policy that clearly defines a net new customer, noting, for instance, that "a $5 net new customer order doesn't qualify for a $500 bonus, but a new customer is defined as an account who hasn't purchased from us in the past two years does qualify."

- **Option 2.** "Every *new* account sold will result in multiplying a bonus factor of 1.25% against the standard commission payout for that contract."

Once you've completed this step, develop an outline for your fiscal year compensation plan, including specific annual objectives and targets.

Step 3: Construct the plan — and create a committee.

With the company goals, basic financial metrics and an outline in your hands, it's time to construct next year's sales compensation plan.

First, select a compensation committee that can advise and assist you. (See Appendix C for three tools designed to help you build your committee, guide its work and roll out the completed plan.)

View your outline as your blueprint, with the committee members acting as "engineers" to help you construct an effective sales compensation plan.

Committee members might include:

- A sales leader (you, as the sales manager)
- A senior sales executive
- A financial analyst
- A compensation administrator
- An administrative assistant

Committee Member Roles

The sales leader has his/her finger on the pulse of the organization, the competition and the marketplace. This person should bring to the table the current requirements for recruiting, motivating and retaining a top-notch sales team—and should also serve as committee chairperson.

The **senior sales executive** brings to the table a review of all compensation items and their effect on the team. This person can provide insights about the potential pitfalls in your plan and how the team will accept it. He or she will also identify the situations where your plans may not achieve the desired results. <u>Guru Tip</u>: This person is key in your rollout strategy. Choose someone you trust, who's viewed as a leader by his or her peers, who has additional leadership potential—and who understands that it's important to be chosen by senior management to help design the team's compensation plan.

The **financial analyst** will run all financial models and reviews. Having this person involved up front saves time and provides a different perspective when discussing ideas. Modeling your various scenarios is critical. This person will have the responsibility to cost-justify the new compensation plan, ensure that it's been calculated properly and review it for other potential problems. The financial analyst will also create the various compensation scenarios depicting sales and commission results that will be used to "sell' the new program to your sales team.

Involving the **compensation administrator**—that is, the person who calculates and pays all commissions -- helps determine whether the plan follows the old maxim of "K.I.S.S." (Keep It Simple, Stupid). An overly complex sales compensation plan will result in salespeople spending too much time figuring out how to get paid rather than focusing on selling, and if such a plan may be too complicated to administer by your accounting department as well.

The **administrative assistant** is responsible for typing, revising and formatting all information and managing the commission policies and commission contracts.

Guru Tip: Work or employment contracts and commission contracts should be separate agreements. A work or employment contract defines a business relationship and covers company policies, such as non-compete rules. The commission contracts simply describe the compensation plan and payment policies. Both agreements must be signed, but the compensation plan can be altered without changing the work contracts. (See Appendix D for examples of compensation agreements.)

Once you've selected your committee, take the following steps to ensure that the group delivers meaningful information to the senior management team:

- Identify the group leader as the focal point between management and the committee.
- Ask the group to establish committee goals and by-laws or rules.
- Have the group review the compensation outline approved by management.
- Set a time frame for delivering the final product. Then work backward to set milestones.

Once everything and everyone is in place, the compensation committee should work toward achieving the following goals:

- Build the final sales compensation plan, including sales position quotas, target income and incentive club criteria.
- Gain the senior management team's approval for the plan.
- Conduct a confidential review of the compensation plan with top sales executives to determine final viability and obtain buy-in. **Guru Tip**: If one top sales executive expresses approval for the plan, others are likely to follow.
- Develop measurable financial metrics for determining the plan's success.
- Establish a quarterly review outline.
- Identify where and when sales contests should be held and recommend how to budget for them.
- Develop a rollout plan for effective implementation.

A successful committee will achieve all its objectives in full and on time.

Step 4: Roll out the plan.

The real test for any compensation plan comes when salespeople first hear and understand the logic behind how they will be paid. The best plan in the world will be only marginally effective if it doesn't include a carefully handled rollout. This must be treated as a selling opportunity by sales leadership.

Guru Tip: Involve your sales compensation committee in planning the implementation. No matter what the size of your company, it's important to educate your entire sales team on three key issues:

1. The company's goals and objectives. Specifically, identify the goals and objectives of the company and address how the plan is designed to help accomplish both.

2. The plan's underlying logic. Address why you designed the plan the way you did.

3. Payment specifics. Spell out how and when salespeople will be paid.

Guru Tip: To hammer home the message that sales compensation is just one component in devising an effective sales strategy, it's also important to discuss the company's "go-to-market" or marketing approach and new sales-support functions before rolling out the sales compensation plan. If the two topics aren't rolled out together, it's likely that people will focus more on the compensation plan than on the overall strategy.

The Implementation Plan

First, create a list of people that you believe need to be educated and informed about the sales compensation plan. Obviously, your list will include the sales team and the compensation administrator, but you may want to include the management team and others as well.

Next, identify the order in which you will educate people about the plan (for example, sales leaders first; entire management team second; sales team third). Now estimate the amount of time needed to educate each group. This step will help you set a timeline.

Next, identify who will present the sales compensation plan. For small companies with one office, the decision is easier than in organizations with multiple locations, which may require several presenters.

Regardless of how many people present the plan, make sure that all speakers deliver the same message. You can accomplish this with a "train-the-trainer" program in which you train all the presenters at once.

Now build the presentation. At a minimum, the presentation should include the following and be presented in the same sequence.

- Overview of company goals and objectives.

- The logic behind the plan.

- An overview of sales strategy and its tie-in to the sales compensation plan.

- Description of marketing programs to support sales objectives.

- Identification of sales compensation committee participants (even if it's just a couple of people), plus identification of the sales executives who provided the final review for the plan.

- Details of the plan, including how and when people will be paid (leave ample time for questions). **Guru Tip**: Make sure you plan logical answers to any potential objections.

- Illustrations of how this year's plan compares to last year's. The more examples and scenarios you provide, the better. Show examples of last year's plan compared to the new plan. Show the high potentials as opposed to the low potential impacts. That helps prevent salespeople from leaving the meeting and immediately beginning to try to "work" the system. It also shows you were careful in analyzing the various scenarios.

Schedule the rollout to occur two to three weeks after the close of your fiscal year. Provide about three weeks' notice for the sales executive presentation, keeping in mind that some executives may well request time off following a strenuous fiscal year. Finally, actually roll out the plan!

Step 5: Review the results.

With the plan in place, it's important to regularly inspect the result. I recommend quarterly reviews to review all established metrics and measure the achievement of goals and objectives.

An organization's financial person should do the analysis and deliver the results to the management team. Once the information has been compiled, schedule a session with the sales team to:

- Detail results based on established metrics, goal and objectives
- Gain insights into what succeeded, what didn't work and why
- Establish a quarterly action plan to improve areas of weakness and enhance areas of strength
- Identify success stories to be used for recognizing support staff
- Rank all salespeople as to their achievement vs the defined goals

A final note for sales leaders at small and midsize businesses: Many sales leaders believe that their companies are too small to need a comprehensive process for developing sales compensation plans. Essentially, they're saying that it's acceptable to have sales by accident, rather than sales by planning. I beg to differ!

This process has worked effectively for companies of all sizes and can work for your organization as well. Remember, you really just apply the following basic steps:

1. Evaluate current compensation plan.
2. Determine company goals.
3. Identify compensation outline.
4. Finalize compensation plan.
5. Implementation plan.
6. Review results quarterly.

In other words, plan your work and work your plan. Once your plan is in place, you'll quickly see strong, consistent, high-quality results.

Critical Things to Remember

- To construct an effective compensation plan, you must build a step-by-step process that covers all necessary bases.

- Before you begin constructing a new plan, spending some time evaluating the current or previous year's plan for good, bad and inconsequential results.

- Build a sales compensation plan that drives results in alignment with the company's goals.

- Create a small compensation committee to help build a thoughtful plan that, again, reflects the company's goals.

- Roll out the plan in a consistent and timely way to gain positive feedback and sales team buy-in.

- Perform periodic measurement checks to ensure that the sales compensation plan is delivering intended results

Activity 11: Chapter 6 Benefit Statement
1. The most important concept I learned in Chapter 6 was:
2. My action steps will be:

7 | FINAL WORDS

Let's close with a few tips on streamlining your plan and a little advice on compensation for sales leadership.

It's important to re-emphasize that any successful compensation plan must be both easy to understand and easy to administer. In many situations, the Guru's team have designed compensation plans that reflect multiple objectives, yet are easily understood and easily managed. Creating complex plans that reflect multiple objectives can confuse your real sales objectives, frustrate your sales team and create headaches for your accounting department.

In some cases, we've simply built a plan to drive monthly sales with a flat commission percentage. In addition, we added a margin component where if the average gross margin percentage for the month on all sales transactions was greater than the preset objective, a bonus percentage commission was paid on the total sales for the month.

For example, for one client, we created a plan that paid 6 percent on all revenue. If the average gross margin earned by the salesperson on all sales was 22 percent, and the monthly margin objective set by management was 18 percent, the salesperson received an additional .5 percent commission on all gross sales.

In this particular situation, the client handled many transactions for the month, some relativity low in volume and others that were considered good-sized orders. The client wanted to ensure that their sales team was focused on overall revenue and that the company received orders from net new clients, which, in most cases, were smaller-revenue orders and perhaps lower-margin-level sales. In this case, the salesperson wasn't penalized in comparison to the larger and higher margin orders from the current customer base and yet retained a focus on net new business.

Bottom line: Creating a compensation plan is a balancing act. It's critical to align the compensation plan with your organization's overall objectives, considering both your organization's complex demands and the need to focus sharply on sales-team and sales-management objectives.

Sales Leadership Compensation

In designing sales-leadership compensation plans, the organization's management team must consider both corporate objectives and sales objectives. This may sound obvious, but the Guru's team has seen some sales-leadership compensation plans that are actually at odds with sales-team objectives. We've also seen plans that aren't aligned with compensation plans for other members of the company's management team.

Compensation plans for sales leadership should address the following issues:

Revenue-margin-growth balance: If salespeople are focused on driving revenues with less focus on margin management, sales leadership should focus on margin management as well as revenue or sales growth. Decisions on this issue hinge on salesperson maturity levels, how much latitude they have on discounting, competitive positioning and profit margins available to the organizations.

In this situation, if the salesperson's compensation was 65 percent based on revenue achievement and 35 percent based on margin protection, sales leadership's compensation plans could be based 40 percent on revenue and 60 percent on margin attainment. In such cases, all "special pricing" or discount decisions require sales management's approval. This requirement also ensures that management is constantly inspecting sales team activity to make sure that salespeople are selling at maximum values. This plan increases sales-management focus on the mantra of "inspecting what you expect" from salespeople.

Sales leadership's compensation plans may include the maintenance of pre-defined sales backlogs. This may be effective for manufacturing or professional service organizations or other organizations that require rigid scheduling of people, materials and other resources in a more complex delivery system.

If the company represents multiple and distinct products and services, then building a sales balance between the various product and service groupings should be considered as a sales-management objective. The sales manager may set a bonus figure if the team achieves 100 percent of quota in each product or service category. A larger bonus or percentage of total compensation for the sales leader would be paid to the sales manager if the entire team achieves 100 percent of each product category. This arrangement can be critical to ensuring that all categories are sold in various quantities. In some cases, this is based upon vendor demands, purchasing resources or personnel requirements.

In some instances, management may wish to emphasize specific product or service categories; if so, the compensation plan should be aligned to achieve that objective. Examples might include new product or service categories or a highly profitable or competitive offering that could win market share. In other cases, management may wish to emphasize add-on capability or loss-leader categories to drive other objectives.

Critical Things to Remember

- For best results, design all sales compensation plans so that they're easy to understand and easy to manage.
- Be sure to align sales-leadership compensation plans with corporate goals, sales-team objectives and other managers' compensation plans.
- In designing sales-leadership compensation plans, consider revenue/margin/growth balance, sales backlog maintenance and the number of and priorities for selling the company's products and services.

Activity 12: Chapter 7 Benefit Statement
1. The most important concept I learned in Chapter 7 was:
2. My action steps will be:

APPENDIX A
COMPENSATION PLAN
ASSESSMENT TOOL

This detailed compensation plan assessment may be completed by the sales manager as an overview, or it can be tailored to be completed by each salesperson using an anonymous survey tool. It can also be used by the compensation planning committee during its review process.

Sales Group: _____

Please rate your agreement with the following statements by circling your answer (1=low, or complete disagreement; 5=high, or complete agreement).

1. You are paid accurately and on a timely basis.   1 2 3 4 5

2. The current plan represents the company's current goals.
                          1 2 3 4 5

3. The current plan is fair.   1 2 3 4 5

4. You feel that your objectives were achievable this year.
                          1 2 3 4 5

5. You feel that your objectives were achievable in past years.
                          1 2 3 4 5

6. To your knowledge, your compensation plan is equal to the industry standard.   1 2 3 4 5

7. To your knowledge, the base salary is equal to the industry standard.   1 2 3 4 5

8. To your knowledge, the commission rate is equal to the industry standard.   1 2 3 4 5

9. To your knowledge, the variable to base compensation is equal to the industry standard.   1 2 3 4 5

10. The company's commissions are high enough to achieve the desired results.   1 2 3 4 5

11. The current compensation plan is simple and easy to understand.   1 2 3 4 5

12. The current compensation plan requires less than one hour per month to check.   1 2 3 4 5

13. The current compensation plan favors all groups equally.
                    1 2 3 4 5

14. The current compensation plan is focused on long-term goals at the expense of short-term goals.   1 2 3 4 5

15. The current compensation plan is focused on short-term goals at the expense of long-term goals.   1 2 3 4 5

16. The current plan has no conflicting objectives.   1 2 3 4 5

17. You exceeded your sales goals for the past year.   1 2 3 4 5

18. Your planned sales contests worked, especially in comparison to their costs.   1 2 3 4 5

19. The plan motivates the company's desired activities.
                    1 2 3 4 5

20. The current plan incents growth more than customer retention.
                    1 2 3 4 5

21. The current plan incents customer retention more than growth.
                    1 2 3 4 5

22. The compensation plan accelerated revenues this year.
                    1 2 3 4 5

23. The plan had no conflicts with other groups' goals. 1 2 3 4 5

24. The current plan isn't overly revenue-focused in comparison to other measures.   1 2 3 4 5

25. The compensation plan is attractive to a potential new hire.
                                                    1 2 3 4 5

26. The existing compensation plan motivates employees to stay with the company rather than seeking employment elsewhere.
                                                    1 2 3 4 5

27. Territory and revenue goals are fairly distributed.   1 2 3 4 5

28. Team goals and compensation have the right balance.
                                                    1 2 3 4 5

29. The current plan encourages and rewards high performance.
                                                    1 2 3 4 5

30. The current plan doesn't reward mediocrity.   1 2 3 4 5

31. The current plan is industry-leading and can attract top performers.   1 2 3 4 5

32. The current plan encourages and rewards team effort.
                                                    1 2 3 4 5

Scoring

160-130	Great results! No changes necessary.
129-95	Minor tweaking may be required.
94-60	Some major issues are occurring.
59 or below	Consider revamping entire plan.

Guru Tip: Your answers to specific questions can be valuable for highlighting compensation issues that you need to address. For instance, if you scored 1 or 2 on Question 11, you may want to consider simplifying your compensation plan so that it's easier to understand.

Questions for Further Analysis

1. What would you change about the current compensation plan?

2. What have you observed about other compensation plans that might be effective at your company?

3. Would paying higher commissions for higher performance yield higher revenues?

4. Does the plan need to better recognize long-term or short-term goals? If so, what compensation and management steps might you take to accomplish that goal?

5. Should certain products or services have different compensation plans?

6. What would be the major differences between those plans?

Company Goal Review and Analysis

1. Define the company's goals for the past year and the next 24 months.

2. Describe specifically how compensation can be used to achieve each goal.

3. List the desired activities of the sales team that can be measured and compared to sales results.

4. Define the CoS equation.

5. Consider whether your company is in a high-growth cycle.

6. Consider whether you have major new product/service launches planned for the time period being analyzed.

7. Consider whether you have multiple products and services to be managed via a compensation plan.

8. Consider any seasonal business or product issues.

9. Consider whether compensation or marketing impact these issues. If so, how?

10. Consider whether the existing compensation plan attracts the type of individuals you require.

APPENDIX B
Senior Account Executive
Description and Commission Plan

This document provides a model for describing a senior salesperson's commission plan, spelling out the related roles, responsibilities and expectations. It should be included as a part of a compensation agreement, which should be separate from an employment agreement.

ROLES

- Senior account executive for the company's [location] branch
- Specialist in selling in assigned territory and accounts
- Active team player on the company's [location] team
- Assistant coach to other employees
- Mature, professional, positive representative

RESPONSIBILITIES

- Participate in weekly one-to-one meetings. Come prepared to discuss:

  ◊ Pipeline
  ◊ Monthly forecast
  ◊ Key issues
  ◊ Sales strategies

- Participate in weekly staff and forecast meetings.

- Adopt a consultative sales approach via proficient knowledge of:

  ◊ Company sales framework and methodology
  ◊ All company products and services
  ◊ Company policies and procedures
  ◊ Company's CRM and reporting systems
  ◊ Company's top three competitors and their sales philosophies

- Participate in a personal development program that includes both internal and external training.

- Become literate in:

  ◊ Microsoft Office applications
  ◊ Customer relationship management (CRM) software and vendor tools
  ◊ Social media, such as LinkedIn and Facebook)

EXPECTATIONS

Achieve more than 100 percent of monthly revenue/margin objective.
Amount = $_____

Achieve more than 100 percent of monthly revenue objective.
Amount = $_____

Achieve more than 100 percent of monthly margin objective.
Amount = $_____ margin

Achieve "5x" 90-day proposal pipeline vs. monthly quota.

Lines = $_____

Margin = $_____

Achieve more than 100 percent of monthly solution sales objective.

Amount = $_____

Achieve _____ new accounts per month.

Achieve _____ contracts of more than 2 years = _____ of at least $_____

Help [branch location] secure _____ percent attrition per month.

Achieve more than 100 percent of administrative objectives, including:

- Nine out of every 10 job packages are _____ percent accurate.

- _____ percent of administrative tasks are done accurately and on time.

APPENDIX C

Compensation
Committee Tools

Following are three tools that can help you choose your compensation planning committee members and guide their work from initial discussions to plan rollout.

Tool #1: Committee Membership, Roles and Responsibilities

Use this list to fill list the names of your compensation-planning committee members and to define each person's specific responsibilities.

Sales Leader:
Specific Responsibilities:

Senior Sales Executive/ Team Rep(s):
Specific Responsibilities:

Financial Analyst:
Specific Responsibilities:

Compensation Administrator:
Specific Responsibilities:

Administrative Assistant:
Specific Responsibilities:

Tool #2: Compensation Plan Checklist

Use this checklist with your compensation-planning committee to discuss all aspects of your new commission plan. As-
sign a compensation secretary to record the individual members' recommendations and full committee's decisions.

1. **Define the compensation plan's purpose and objectives.** Consider:
a. Maturity of company: Rate it 1-5 (where 5=very mature)
b. Maturity of industry: Rate it 1-5 (where 5= very mature)

2. **Define all relevant goals.**
- Define overall company goals.
- Define your division's goals.
- Define the sales organization's goals.
- Define your recruiting and retention goals.
- Define the objectives of a new compensation plan.
- Define the goals of existing and new products and ser-
  vices.

3. **Consider salespeople's profiles.**

Are you compensating a "hunter" or a "farmer" sales profile?
You may require multiple compensation plans, or you may
need to combine certain aspects based on your sales organization's structure and your company's customer base.

4. **Choose the components for the plan's foundation.**

First, answer these questions: On what factor should the plan
be primarily based: Revenue volume? Gross Margin Gener-

ated Profit margins percentage? Can the compensation plan include both options? Should customer satisfaction be included as a factor?

Then consider one additional question: Can the salesperson control the gross or net profit? If margin is the dominant factor in the compensation plan, the salesperson must have certain levels of control in managing the profit margin. Salespeople may have limits over costs or discount levels; however, if other departments are controlling other aspects of delivery that impact potential costs or margins, then the plan isn't sound.

In many organizations, sales management controls most margin/profit decisions; for that reason, their compensation is more heavily weighted to P&L responsibility and margin percentage attainment. **Guru Tip**: Consider bonus plans, sales contests, products, services, promotions and stock options as part of total compensation.

Key Considerations

1. Know the cost of sales (CoS). Consider:

- **Fixed costs**, including fixed salaries, cell phone expenses and car allowances.

- **Variable costs**, including commissions paid.

- **Marketing costs**, typically based upon the total marketing budget, telemarketing costs, sales support, number of salespeople and the programs focused on lead generation.

2. **Understand the sales cycle. Consider:**

• **Length of time:** Short or transactional sales cycles point to compensation plans based upon weekly or monthly achievements. Longer sales cycles may include quarterly or annual target levels.

• **Degree of challenge:** Early-stage companies, or those with new or leading-edge products and services, require both the right combination of salespeople and compensation plans that can "create orders." In past situations, with early stage organizations we have created compensation plans that were based upon "new order patterns." Mature organizations with market-share dominance can afford to pay lower overall compensation levels.

Guru Tip: In some situations involving early-stage/leading-edge organizations, compensation may be paid on orders rather than invoices or customer payments.

3. **Determine the time frame for your plan.**

• **Six months or 12 months:** I recommend avoiding changing sales-compensation plans purely for the sake of change. If it works, great. If it doesn't, fix it.

Consider six-month plans work if your market is growing extremely rapidly or if your company is in a tenuous financial situation. These shorter plans are fair to both the sales team and management as both are unsure of the future. For the vast number of organizations building stability into compensation, long-term planning is the best policy.

Tool #3: Committee Checklist for Compensation Plan Rollout

Your committee should agree to actions defined below and complete them by the date specified. You may want to consider assigning specific responsibilities or tasks to individual committee members or to others in your organization.

Provide all those involved in planning with relevant information, such as relevant portions of your compensation presentation, documents detailing management's commitments to the sales team and comparisons of the proposed, current and past compensation plans. The documents must be easy to understand and clearly show the reasons and benefits of the proposed plan. They should also spell out all policies about commissions, payment and sales contests.

Guru Tip: In preparing your timeline, start with the proposed rollout date and work backward to the first step: reviewing the existing plan.

Action	Assigned To	Complete By
☐ Plan rolled out to sales team	_____	_____
☐ Final senior management review	_____	_____
☐ Rehearsal for roll-out	_____	_____
☐ Final preparation of all handouts	_____	_____
☐ Management sign-off on plan/handouts	_____	_____
☐ Approval by compensation committee	_____	_____
☐ Final financial review	_____	_____
☐ Final plan recommendation	_____	_____
☐ Completion of planning work	_____	_____
☐ Definition of corporate goals	_____	_____
☐ Review of existing plan	_____	_____

APPENDIX D
Examples of Compensation Agreements

Following are three examples of compensation agreements. You may want to consider adopting some of the language and provisions into your own compensation planning.

Compensation Agreement #1

Acumen Management Ltd. Compensation Plan

ACCOUNT EXECUTIVE

I. Purpose

To achieve Acumen Management Inc.'s goals for growth and profitability by motivating our sales personnel to meet and exceed set sales objectives.

II. Effective Date

The Plan is effective [month, day, year] and will remain in effect until [month, day, year] unless superseded, modified, or terminated prior to that time by the Company. Acumen Management Inc. (the "Company") has the right to terminate or modify this document at any time with or without notice and without further compensation to the employee. The Plan will apply to invoices generated/commissions paid between [month, day, year] and [month, day, year].

III. Eligibility

Acumen Management Inc. Account Executives who market applications, products, and services, and who are selected by the Company in writing, are eligible to participate in the Plan. No participant in the Plan will participate in any other sales or bonus compensation plan of the Company.

IV. Territory Assignments

Each Account Executive will have a list of accounts for which they will provide services, products and support. There will be a master list of accounts that will be provided to all account managers. Each account managed by an Account Executive will be protected, provided that sales activity has been recorded within 120 days. If an account asks to change Account Executive for any reason, all compensation from that day forward will be rewarded to the new Account Executive. Some accounts will be assigned to the Company.

Territorial boundaries will be established for some Account Executives, which will constitute a Territory for the Account Executive. For the purposes of this Compensation Plan, any products sold within an Account Executive's Territory will belong to the Account Executive; however, any sales from accounts that have been assigned to another Account Executive or are Company accounts shall belong to the assigned Account Executive or the Company regardless of the Territory in which the sales took place. Territorial boundaries may be changed or eliminated at any time in the sole discretion of the Company. The Company may also establish new offices throughout the country; current accounts may be assigned to these offices.

In all cases, the Company may, in its sole discretion, reassign accounts to other Territories and/or Account Executives, with or without cause or notice, and compensation from that day forward will be awarded to the new Account Executive/ Territory, or to the Company if not reassigned.

V. Code of Conduct/Business Ethics

Account Executives are required to submit information to management such as forecasts, call sheets, contact information, and related information as requested by the Company. Account Executives will at all times represent the Company in an honest and ethical manner and shall not engage in any misrepresentation of fact, pricing, or capabilities of product, or otherwise compromise the integrity or reputation of the Company. In addition, any activity such as stealing Company property, misleading customers, or engaging in conduct contrary to the image that Acumen Management Inc. desires is strictly prohibited.

Violations of this provision may result in corrective action, up to and including immediate dismissal.

VI. Sales Meetings

Monthly sales meeting will be held and all Account Executives are expected to attend. The time and place will be announced each month. These meetings are an important barometer, measuring how successful the Company is in meeting its current and future goals and objectives. These monthly meetings will be used for product training, sales training, team building exercises, and other important topics and issues.

We will have sales meetings at [time] every [day of week] unless canceled in advance. We may also schedule meetings at other times as needed. These meetings are crucial to our success. As such, failure to be on time or otherwise attend these meetings may result in corrective action.

VII.   Product Commission

"Product" is defined as hardware, software and services purchased from another vendor.

Product Commission will be paid as a percentage of
"Gross Profit" as reflected below. Gross Profit will be deter-
mined by subtracting "Total Costs" from "Total Gross Sales
Revenue."

Gross profit % on sale	Commission rate
0.00 to 4.99	00%
5.00 and over	20%

For purposes of calculating Product Commission, "Total
Gross Sales Revenue" will mean the amount invoiced for
hardware, software, and services sold and identified on the
Company's sales order. No other charges or fees, such as
freight, taxes, miscellaneous charges, and the like, will be included in determining Total Gross Sales Revenue, and thus
will not qualify for order credit or commission credit. "Total
Costs" will include, without limitation, all costs on invoices
from vendors, as well as any other cost item that is charge-
able to a particular sale.

Example 1: The customer invoice totals $97,000. This includes
$75,000 for computer hardware, $10,000 for software, $5,000
for services, maintenance, $6,000 in sales taxes and $1,000 for
freight. Costs for the computer hardware, software, and services maintenance are $90,350. The commission on this in-
voice is calculated as follows:

	Revenue	Costs	Profit	Commis-sion
Hardware	75,000	70,000	5,000	1,000
Software	10,000	9,600	400	0
Services	5,000	3,750	1,250	250
Taxes	6,000	6,000	0	0
Freight	1,000	1,000	0	0
TOTAL	$97,000	$90,350	$ 6,650	$1,250

Products that are sold and not drop-shipped to the customer will be subject to a delivery fee that will be added as a cost to the transaction.

Any sale with a Gross Profit of less than 5% will need to be approved in advance and in writing by management. Failure to obtain such timely approval may result in the non-payment of corresponding commission.

Gross profit will be calculated on each individual line item on the invoice.

VIII.   Services Commission

"Service" is defined as services provided by Acumen Management employees. Service commissions will be paid at the following rates:

Gross Profit will be determined by subtracting "Total Cost" from "Total Gross Sales Revenue." Revenue will be determined by subtracting items such as; sales tax, special insurance, performance bonds and any other direct costs that are not marked up by the company from the total revenue. All costs associated with subcontractors required to perform a project will be subtracted from the gross revenue to determine commissions.

Service	Gross Profit List	Revenue List
Time & Materials	25%	-
Fixed Cost Projects	20%	-
Maintenance Contracts (See note on Renewals)	-	10%/5%
Cabling	20%	-
Blocks of Time	-	10%

For the purposes of calculating "Time and Materials", "Fixed Cost Project" commissions, and "Structured Cabling" "Gross Profit" is defined as Total Gross Sales Revenue less the cost of goods sold and expenses directly associated to the project that are not paid for by the customers, i.e. expenses, taxes, miscellaneous parts, etc.

For the purposes of calculating "Maintenance Contracts" commissions, "Revenue" is defined as Total Gross Sales less expenses directly associated to the project that are not paid for by the customers, i.e. taxes, special insurance, etc. Commission on renewals of "Maintenance Contracts" will be paid at 5% of Revenue. Commission earned may also be reduced on Maintenance Contracts that are sold at discounted rates. All "Maintenance Contract" pricing must be approved by the Vice President of Services. Sales persons will receive commissions on Maintenance Contracts and Blocks of time only after the customer has paid the invoice.

Example 1: The customer invoice totals $100,000. This includes $50,000 for installation services on a time and materials basis, $40,000 for Cabling, $10,000 for a Maintenance contract. Commission would be calculated as follows:

	Revenue	Costs	Profit	Commis-sion
Services - T&M	50,000	30,000	20,000	5,000
Cabling	40,000	26,000	14,000	2,800
Mainte-nance	10,000	7,500	2,500	1,000
TOTAL	$100,000	$63,500	$36,500	$8,800

Example 2: The customer invoice totals $200,000. This in-cludes $50,000 for a block of time, $50,000 for professional services on a T&M basis, $50,000 of structured cabling servic-es, and a $50,000 maintenance contract. Commission would be calculated as follows:

	Revenue	Costs	Profit	Commis-sion
Block of Time	50,000	25,000	25,000	5,000
Services - T&M	50,000	30,000	20,000	4,000
Cabling	50,000	20,000	30,000	6,000
Mainte-nance	50,000	37,500	12,500	5,000
TOTAL	$200,000	$112,500	$ 87,500	$20,000

It is important for Acumen Management Inc. to make a profit on all Blocks of Time, Time and Material Projects, Fixed Cost Projects, Cabling and Maintenance Contracts/Service Level Agreements. Management will establish the service rates and pricing. If the project or maintenance contract were sold at management-established rates, commission would be paid at the pricing schedule listed above.

Acumen Management Inc. realizes it is necessary at times to discount established rates in a competitive situation. When the established rates are discounted for a project or maintenance contract the commission as listed above may be reduced in proportion to the discounted rate. Commission rates on discounted blocks of time or projects must be determined and approved prior to the beginning of the engagement. It is the responsibility of the salesperson to obtain authorization of discounted rates and commission structure on those discounted rates.

IX. Recoverable Draw Program

The Company may, at its discretion, advance funds to certain Account Executives in lieu of future commissions in the form of recoverable "Draws." The amount and frequency of such Draws will be determined by the Company in writing, but will normally be paid bi-weekly.

> All gross Draw payments (i.e., gross payment before taxes and any other withholdings) made to each Account Executive will be accounted for by the Company on an ongoing, cumulative basis, creating a "Draw Balance" for each participating Account Executive. Any Product or Services Commissions thereafter payable to the Account Executive will first be applied against any outstanding Draw Balance the employee may have on the date the Commission payment is due and payable.

> The maximum Draw Balance is $6,000. Therefore, full Draw payments will not be made that would put a Draw Balance in excess of this amount. In such a case, Draw payments will be suspended until the Draw Balance is reduced accordingly, at which time Draw payments will

resume according to the Account Executive's normal schedule.

Draws are intended to be advances against future commissions and, as such, are not intended to be additional compensation. Therefore, the minimum Draw Balance is zero ($0) dollars, and employees are not entitled to any type of compensation or credit for any "negative" Draw Balances.

Example 1: An employee is eligible to receive a monthly commission check in the gross amount of $1,600, but has an outstanding Draw Balance of $1,000 on the date he/she is scheduled to receive the commission check. Therefore, the employee will be entitled to a commission check in the gross amount (before taxes and other withholdings) of $600 ($1,600 - $1,000) on the date the commission check is due, and the employee's Draw Balance will be reduced to $0. The $0 Draw Balance will thereafter increase by the gross amount of the next Draw payment made to the employee.

Example 2: An employee is eligible to receive a monthly commission check in the gross amount of $600, but has an outstanding Draw Balance of $1,000 on the date he/she is scheduled to receive the commission check. Therefore, the employee's Draw Balance will be reduced to $400 ($1,000 - $600), and the employee will not receive a commission check at that time. The $400 Draw Balance will thereafter increase by the gross amount of the next Draw payment made to the employee.

All gross sums paid in the form of Draws are considered advances from the Company to the employee in lieu of future commissions. All Commission and Draw payments shall be considered compensation that is subject to withholdings when paid.

X. Payment of Commissions

Commissions on product or services that are paid as percentage of "Gross Profit" will be calculated upon completion of the work, after all cost have been captured and the customer has been invoiced.

Commissions will be paid, net of Draw, on the 20th of the month following invoice date. Commissions will only be paid to the extent that they exceed the cumulative year-to-date Draw Balance.

It is our desire that Commission payments are accurate, and Account Executives are urged to review their Commission payments, as well as their cumulative Draw Balances, promptly upon receipt to ensure accuracy. We will gladly work with you to explain or resolve any questions or problems you may have. Any such problems or questions must be brought to the attention of your sales manager or other member of management within 30 days of payment, as extended periods make it difficult to trace and resolve the problem and may lead to further problems or inaccuracies in the future.

XI. Cash With Order

Sales people will receive and additional ½% commission on all orders in which the customer prepays the order. The additional ½% will be added to the normal commission rate and will be calculated accordingly.

Gross Profit Goal will be the calendar year total of the monthly Gross Profits, as the term defined in Sections VII and VIII above.

XII. **General**

This Plan is intended to provide an incentive to and to reward Account Executives for not only the quantity of sales they achieve, but also for providing quality service over the course of the business relationship with the customer and helping to generate an overall long-term, positive image for the Company. In order to achieve these goals, it will necessary for the Company to review this Plan on an ongoing basis and to make any revisions necessary to better achieve these goals, up to and including the elimination of the Plan. As such, nothing in this Plan is intended to create an express or implied contract for any purpose or is intended as a limitation on the Company's ability to revise or eliminate the Plan at any time, with or without notice or cause. The Plan is also not intended to create a contract for employment or otherwise affect in any manner the Account Executive's status, as an employee at will.

If an Account Executive's employment voluntarily or involuntarily ends for any reason, or if the Account Executive is placed in another position with the Company that is not covered by the Plan, he/she will be paid, net of any outstanding Draw Balance due on the date of separation, commissions due on items invoiced up to the date of separation, and one-half of commissions due on fully-completed and approved items that have been received in-hand as of the date of separation but not yet invoiced. In all cases, he/she will not be entitled to any commissions or other compensation that would have normally become due after the 20th of the calendar month following separation.

This document and any documents relating hereto, as well as the information contained in this and other such documents, are all considered to be the property of the Company. As such, the documents and information are to be treated as trade secrets and confidential and are not to be divulged in any manner, directly or indirectly, to third parties by employees or former employees of the Company without specific permission in writing to do so.

Accepted by: _____

Date: _____

Compensation Agreement #2

This is another example of a company's commission policy and compensation plan agreement.

_____ **Company Commission Plan Policy Document**

Purpose

The intent of this document is to describe the structure and policies surrounding the [Company Name] compensation program. This document will be used as the general guidelines as to how Account Executives are paid for sales performance.

Term

This document will be effective on [month, day year] and remain effective until the last day of the [Company Name] sales year in [month, year].

Quota

[Company Name] has a quota expectation for each [Company Name] Account Executive of $2,000,000 in collected revenue to the organization within [sales year].

The Program

General Commission Structure: [Company Name] sales professionals will be paid 4% of gross revenue for software and services they sell and that are paid for. Upon achieving quota ($2M of collected revenue) the percentage of commission paid off of gross revenue collected will increase to 7%. In addition, bonuses will be paid based on certain levels of revenue collected.

The following is a depiction of the percentage of commission paid in relation to revenue produced.

Gross Software and Services Revenue	Commission %
$500,000	4%
$1,000,000	4%
$1,500,000	4%
$2,000,000	4%
Revenue > $2,000,000	7%

Total Revenue Tier Bonuses		Tier Bonus $
Tier I:	$500,000	$5,000
Tier II:	$1,000,000	$10,000
Tier III:	$1,500,000	$15,000
Tier IV:	$2,000,000	$20,000

Example of Commission Earnings

1. At $500,000 in revenue collected by [Company Name] in association with an Account Executive's direct selling activities, the corresponding Account Executive would earn $25,000 in commission. The following is a breakdown of how that would occur:

   Revenue Collected ($500,000) x Commission Percentage (4%) + Revenue Tier I Bonus Level ($5,000) = $25,000.

2. At $1,000,000 in revenue collected by [Company Name] in association with an Account Executive's direct selling activities, the corresponding Account Executive would earn $55,000 in commissions. The following is a break-down of how that would occur:

   Revenue Collected ($1,000,000) x Commission Percent-age (4%) + Revenue Tier I & II Bonus Levels ($15,000) = $55,000.

3. At $2,000,000 in revenue collected by [Company Name] in association with an Account Executive's direct selling activities, the corresponding Account Executive would earn $130,000 in commissions. The following is a break-down of how that would occur:

   Revenue Collected ($2,000,000) x Commission Percentage (4%) + Revenue Tier I, II, III & IV Bonus Levels ($50,000) = $130,000.

4. At $3,000,000 in revenue collected by [Company Name] in association with an Account Executive's direct selling activities, the corresponding Account Executive would earn $200,000 in commissions. The following is a break-down of how that would occur:

   Revenue Collected Post Quota ($1,000,000) x Commis-sion Percentage (7%) + Software Commission Earning at Quota (80,000, bonus dollars not applicable) + Tier I, II, III & IV Bonus Levels ($50,000) = $200,000.

Policy Statements

This program is based on revenue collected by [Company Name] association with sales efforts. Therefore, revenue sold, but not collected is not commissionable, nor will it be applied toward revenue tiers associated with bonuses.

Revenue collected toward the tiered bonuses depicted above will begin on the first day and end on the last day of SY__. Therefore, if services revenue is collected after the end of SY__, those revenues will be credited toward the following sales year, regardless of when they were sold.

[Company Name] reserves the right to alter this program or institute a different program following SY__. In those circumstances, the organization will work to do what is fair and reasonable for all Account Executives under the current plan, but no specific guarantees are implied herein.

[Company Name] management also reserves the right to alter this program based on any unique custom or special sales opportunities developed by [Company Name], our partners, or the sales persons.

As a general rule, sales professionals will be compensated for services sold in association with a specific project for one year from the date of sale. If a project is sold that is anticipated to require services that will span longer than one calendar year, the sales professional does have the right to petition with their Regional Lead and the National Sales Lead to receive some level of compensation beyond this timeframe. Note that this in no way implies a commitment on behalf of [Company Name] to pay services beyond one year.

Under general circumstances, Account Executives will have the ability to sell into new business accounts for 6 months from the date of sale. At that time all sales activities into these accounts will be assumed by the corresponding CPM in the Region. Account Executives will have the ability to name up to 3 customers as "Key Accounts." Any account is eligible to be named as a "Key Account" upon approval from the corresponding Regional Lead.

Recurring revenue, specifically software enhancement renewals, are not commissionable.

Commissions will only be paid to [Company Name] sales professionals for transactions they had an active role in bringing to closure.

The commission plan represented in this document only pertains to software orders at an overall margin of 30% or more to [Company Name]. [Company Name] management reserves the right to not pay out commission as depicted herein for software orders below this percentage of margin. It will be at the discretion of the Regional Lead and National Sales Lead as to the appropriate percentage to be paid for orders that fall under circumstances such as this.

Clarifications

The information contained herein pertains only to commissions and is considered potential earnings above and beyond the individual base salaries of [Company Name] Account Executives.

There is no cap established for potential commission earning. While the examples above exemplify potential earnings up to $3M in revenue produced, [Company Name] Account Executives will continue to earn the standard commission percentage if their revenue performance exceeds this amount.

Payment Policies

All commissions will be paid on the second payroll of the month. Cash must be received by the close of the prior month to be paid the month following.

Commission payments will be made based on revenue collected. Therefore in situations where special terms are negotiated for software purchased, 100% collection of software payment is not needed for commission to be paid. Instead, sales professionals will be paid the appropriate percentage of commission based on the amount of each payment as it is collected.

Acceptance

Your signature below is representative that you have evaluated the contents of this document and feel as though you have a thorough understanding of the [Company Name] SY__ Compensation Plan delineated herein.

Your signature below also exemplifies that you understand the quota expectations associated with your specific role as a [Company Name] Sales Professional. The lack of quota achievement can result in a formal review process and, ultimately, dismissal.

It is a pleasure having you as part of the [Company Name] National Sales Team. Rest assured that you are part of something special.

Very truly yours,

[Hiring executive's name]
[Hiring executive's title]
_____(Hiring executive's signature)

Agreed to, and accepted by:

_____ (Employee's signature)

_____ (Employee's printed name)

_____ (Date)

Compensation Agreement #3

This is example depicts a simplified — yet still complete-- compensation plan that Acumen Management has provided to its clients.

Compensation Plan for [Company Name]

This purpose of this agreement is to define the compensation plan between [Company Name] located at _____, and the below-signed employee. Schedule A is attached and considered part of this agreement.

Understandings:

- Employee is considered a full-time employee and will only perform similar services for Company.

- Employee is qualified for all benefits and plans associated with being a full-time employee of Company.

- All commissions paid are due based upon the attached schedule and upon payment from Company's client.

- Employee agrees to sign Company's nondisclosure/confidentiality/non-compete Statements.

- Company retains the right to alter Schedule A on a six-month basis.

- Company and Employee agree that any unique or custom potential sales contracts may require a commission schedule different from the attached schedule. All such commission agreements will be determined prior to Company's formal client contractual agreement.

☐ Employee agrees to submit forecasts, account reporting, attend trade shows, attend company related events and perform other duties related to the success of the company as reasonably requested by Management of Company.

☐ Company agrees to pay all commissions and bonus payments promptly and according to the terms defined in Schedule A. All commissions will be paid on the first payroll of each month on all qualified and paid customer invoices.

Signed: _____ (Company Signature)

Agreed: _____ (Employee Signature)

Printed Name: _____

Date: _____

Schedule A

Commission Plan

Name: _____

Position: _____

Contract Commission: _____ %

Payment is on the first payroll of each month and after receipt of customer payment.

APPENDIX E
Additional Compensation Plan Tools, Concepts and Examples

Sample Goal Sheet

FY _____

GOALS

Name: _____ Title: <u>Sales Executive</u>

Goal #1 of 5   Weight: 45%

Achieve Sales/Bookings and Margin Objective

Weight	Measurement Criteria	Fully Achieving	Over-Achieving
50%	Achieve "$x" margin per month	90 –104%	105%+
50%	Achieve "$x" sales per month	90 –104%	105%+

Goal #2 of 5   Weight: 15%

Achieve "5x" Pipeline Objective

Weight	Measurement Criteria	Fully Achieving	Over-Achieving
50%	Total margin proposal pipeline of "$x" (5x) for 90-day time frame	90 –104%	105%+
50%	Total sales proposal pipeline of "$x" (5x) for 90-day time frame	90 –104%	105%+

Goal #3 of 5   Weight: 15%

Achieve Solution Sales Monthly Objective

Weight	Measurement Criteria	Fully Achieving	Over-Achieving
	Additional products sold monthly		
40%	Application #1 (new product sales; 2 customers sign contracts	2	3+
40%	Application #2 = 80% of all service contracts renewed	80%	90%+
20%	Application #3 = TBD		

Goal #4 of 5   Weight: 15%

Achieve New Account Objective

Weight	Measurement Criteria	Fully Achieving	Over-Achieving
100%	Sell 2 new accounts each month	2 Accounts	3+ Accounts

Goal #5 of 5   Achieve Company/Team Customer Attrition
Weight: 10%   Objective

Weight	Measurement Criteria	Fully Achieving	Over-Achieving
100%	Fewer than 5% of company customers no longer do business with company	5%	More than 5%

Sales Executive: _____

Date: _____

Sales Manager: _____

Date: _____

Other Compensation Concepts

If your organization offers a variety of physical products and a professional consulting service that you could offer separately or in combined packages, your compensation plan may need to offer combinations based on the margin of the product sales and revenue-based compensation for the professional services.

In the example below, you will find a combination of salary, an overhead contribution of 35 percent and an accelerated plan with three levels of revenue attainment and commission percentage. The first break point is up to $400,000 in sales with a 10 percent commission that accelerates to 20 percent at the maximum levels.

The second half of the compensation plan adds an accelerated plan on product margins, with the first break point starting at up to $180,000 at 20 percent commission. The total CoS is 9.8 percent.

Sales Compensation Plan

Sales Executive

Base salary	$	65,000
Payroll overhead		35%
Annual fixed selling cost	$	87,750

		% Comm	Sales Range (000s)	
Commission Structure on Direct Sales				
Service Sales on Revenue			$0-to	
Commissions Level 1	$ 40,000	10%	$ 400K	0-400
Commissions Level 2	$ 15,000	15%	$ 100K	400-500
Commissions Level 3	$ 20,000	20%	$ 100K	500+

Appendix E

Total Potential Commissions Paid	$ 75,000
Total Sales for Year	$ 600
Annualized Sales	$ 600

Product Commission in Margin Dollars
(assumed margin)   15%

Commission Level 1	$ 36,000	20%	$180	Up to 180,000
Commission Level 2	$ 19,800	33%	$ 60	180-240
Commission Level 3	$ 20,000	40%	$ 50	240-+

Total Potential Commissions Paid $ 75,800

		Margin/Revenue
Total Margin Generated	$ 290	666%

Annualized Sales	$ 2,531,400
Total commissions	$ 50,800
Fixed selling costs	$ 87,750
(salary, benefits, travel)	

Total cost of selling to Company $ 238,550 9.4%   Cost of sales
Sales Compensation (no overhead) $ 215,800 8.5%   Cost of sales

Maintenance Sales	$ 40,000	10%	$ 400
	$ 2,000	20%	$ 100
Total Maintenance Commissions	$ 60,000		$ 500

Grand Total of Potential Commissions	$ 210,800

Fixed Costs of Selling $ 87,750

Total Compensation	$298,550	9.8%	Cost of Sales

You may also consider month-to-month compensation plans to drive short-term sales focus. In the example below, you see a salary with a 35 percent overhead allocation. Each month has a target of $60,000 in professional services with a standard commission percentage, with a bonus commission on all sales of more than $60,000, retroactively. This means that all sales greater than $60,000, plus the original $60,000, will earn the bonus commission.

The second half of the plan is based on product sales with a monthly objective of $5,000 of gross margin with an accelerated bonus commission if the salesperson attains the $5,000 objective.

You will also notice a built-in quarterly bonus. I recommend that, when you're building monthly focused sales compensation plans, you build in quarterly objectives with bonus opportunities. The reason: It helps keep salespeople focused. If individuals fall short one month, they can make up the difference in income when the quarterly objective is attained.

Appendix E

Sales Compensation Plan

Sales Base salary	$ 55,000
Payroll overhead	35%
Annual fixed selling cost	$ 74,250

Commission Structure on Services						
Monthly Sales 2011	100% Target Commission	% Comm	Revenue Goal $0 to M	Monthly Growth 15%	Bonus	Comm
Jan	$3600	6%	$60K	$9K	4%	$360
Feb	$3600	6%	$60K	$9K	4%	$360
March	$3600	6^	$60K	$9K	4%	$360
April	$3600	6%	$60K	$9K	4%	$360
May	$3600	6%	$60K	$9K	4%	$360
June	$3600	6%	$60K	$9K	4%	$360
July	$3600	6%	$60K	$9K	4%	$360
Aug	$3600	6%	$60K	$9K	4%	$360
Sept	$3600	6%	$60K	$9K	4%	$360
Oct	$3600	6%	$60K	$9K	4%	$360
Nov	$3600	6%	$60K	$9K	4%	$360
Dec	$3600	6%	$60K	$9K	4%	$360
Monthly Potential Comm Paid	$43,200					
Total Sales for Year			$720K	$108K	$6480	$4320
Annualized Sales for Services	$720K					$828K
Total Potential Comm Paid	$54K					

Commission Structure on Products						
Monthly Sales 2011	100% Target Comm	% Comm	Margin Goal $0 to M	Monthly Growth 15%	Bonus	Comm
Jan	$250	5%	$5K	$750	4%	$30
Feb	$250	5%	$5K	$750	4%	$30
March	$250	5%	$5K	$750	4%	$30
April	$250	5%	$5K	$750	4%	$30
May	$250	5%	$5K	$750	4%	$30
June	$250	5%	$5K	$750	4%	$30
July	$250	5%	$K	$750	4%	$30
Aug	$250	5%	$5K	$750	4%	$30
Sept	$250	5%	$5K	$750	4%	$30
Oct	$250	5%	$5K	$750	4%	$30
Nov	$250	5%	$5K	$750	4%	$30
Dec	$250	5%	$5K	$750	4%	$30
Total Potential Comm Paid	$3000		$60K			
Total Sales for Year			$30M	$9K	$450	$360
Annualized Sales	$729K					>$30M
Potential Comm on Products	$3810					
	$ 57,810	8.029%			20%	
Quarterly Bonus						
1st Qtr	$4,500					

Commission Structure on Products						
Monthly Sales 2011	100% Target Comm	% Comm	Margin Goal $0 to M	Monthly Growth 15%	Bonus	Comm
2nd Qtr	$4500					
3rd Qtr	$4500					
4th Qtr	$4500					
Salary	$55,000					
Total Potential Income	$130,810	17.94%				

Acumen

Management Group, Ltd.

Building organizations
through the execution of
strategic sales management

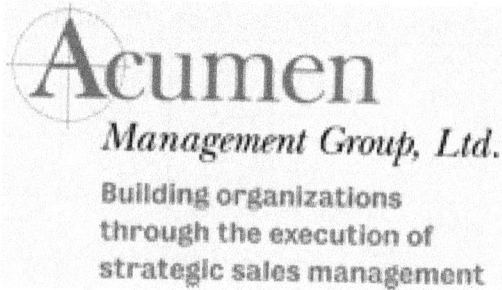

Contact Ken Thoreson

165 Golanvyi Trail, Vonore, TN 37885

(423) 884-6328

Website: www.AcumenManagement.com

Email: Ken@AcumenMgmt.com

Blog: www.YourSalesManagementGuru.com

**Purchase the entire Your Sales Management Guru's
Guide Series at:**

http://YourSalesManagementGuru.SalesGravy.com

About the Author

Ken Thoreson, Acumen Management Group, Ltd. president, is a sales leadership professional who "operationalizes" sales management systems and processes to pull sales results out of the doldrums into the fresh zone of predictable revenue. The sales management thought leader is recognized as an expert in sales execution, channel management, revenue generation, sales analysis, compensation, forecasting, recruitment, and training within the sales function. Over the past 12 years, his consulting, advisory, and platform services have illuminated, motivated, and rejuvenated the sales efforts for companies throughout North America—from emerging , transitional to high-growth. Prior to founding Acumen, he led development-stage, entrepreneurial, and $250-million national vertical software sales organizations as vice president of sales.

As a speaker, Ken energizes audiences and recharges their personal commitment to professional excellence to help drive personal and organizational change and growth. He is a member of The National Speakers Association.

In addition to the two books he has authored and the Sales Management Guru series, Ken's many articles and nationally recognized blog are excellent resources for executives who want to revitalize their organizations. He has been published in Selling Power, VARBusiness, Reseller Management, Business Products Professional and SmartReseller. He is currently a columnist for Redmond Channel Partner Magazine, a publication for Microsoft channel partners.

www.ingramcontent.com/pod-product-compliance
Lightning Source LLC
Chambersburg PA
CBHW031811190326
41518CB00006B/288